# On Improvisation

## Nine Conversations with Roberto Ciulli

P.I.E.-Peter Lang

Bruxelles · Bern · Berlin · Frankfurt/M · New York · Oxford · Wien

# Dramaturgies

Texts, Cultures and Performances

**Series Editor**

Marc Maufort, *Université Libre de Bruxelles*

**Editorial Board**

Christopher Balme, *University of Mainz*
Judith E. Barlow, *State University of New York-Albany*
Johan Callens, *Vrije Universiteit Brussel*
Jean Chothia, *Cambridge University*
Harry J. Elam, *Stanford University*
Albert-Reiner Glaap, *University of Düsseldorf*
André Helbo, *Université Libre de Bruxelles*
Ric Knowles, *University of Guelph*
Alain Piette, *École d'interprètes internationaux-Mons/ Université Catholique de Louvain*
John Stokes, *King's College, University of London*
Joanne Tompkins, *University of Queensland-Brisbane*

**Editorial Assistant**

Franca Bellarsi, *Université Libre de Bruxelles*

Malgorzata BARTULA &
Stefan SCHROER

# On Improvisation

## Nine Conversations with Roberto Ciulli

Translated by Geoffrey V. Davis

Dramaturgies
No.12

These conversations took place between February 1998 and April 2000

The authors wish to thank Geoffrey V. DAVIS for his invaluable help and patience

Photographs, layout and text formatting by Robert SCHATTON

No part of this book may be reproduced in any form, by print, photocopy, microfilm or any other means, without prior written permission from the publisher. All rights reserved.

© P.I.E.-Peter Lang s.a., Presses Interuniversitaires Européennes,
Brussels, 2003
1 avenue Maurice, 1050 Brussels, Belgium
info@peterlang.com, www.peterlang.net

ISSN 1376-3199
ISBN 90-5201-185-0
D/2003/5678/17

*CIP available from the British Library, GB and the Library of Congress, USA.*
*ISBN 0-8204-6604-2*

Bibliographic information published by "Die Deutsche Bibliothek"
"Die Deutsche Bibliothek" lists this publication in the "Deutsche Nationalbibliografie"; detailed bibliographic data is avalaible in the Internet at <http://dnb.ddb.de>.

Tosto sarà che a veder queste cose
non ti fia grave, ma fieti diletto
quanto natura a sentir ti dispuose[1]

Dante Alighieri

Wir sind keine Humanitarier;
wir würden uns nie zu erlauben wagen,
von unsrer "Liebe zur Menschheit" zu reden –
dazu ist unsereins nicht Schauspieler genug![2]

Friedrich Nietzsche

---

[1] Dante, *The Divine Comedy: Purgatory*. Canto XV, lines 31-33. Translation: "Not long from now, a sight like this will prove / to be no burden, but a joy as great / as Nature has prepared your soul to feel". (Translated by Mark Musa, Bloomington: Indiana University Press, 1981).

[2] Translation: "We are no humanitarians; we should never dare to permit ourselves to speak of our 'love of humanity'; our kind is not actor enough for that" (*The Gay Science*, transl. Walter Kaufmann [New York: Vintage Books, 1974], p.339).

# Table of Contents

**First Conversation**
Freedom in Prison .................................................... 11

**Second Conversation**
The Age of Apes......................................................... 27

**Third Conversation**
A Better Prison ........................................................... 37

**Fourth Conversation**
Life Is the Most Difficult Art ..................................... 51

**Fifth Conversation**
Life Belongs to the Actor .......................................... 61

**Sixth Conversation**
Working on the Creation of Something New
in the Green Fields .................................................... 69

**Seventh Conversation**
Theatre for the Outsider............................................. 75

**Eighth Conversation**
Myself as a Member of the Audience........................ 87

**Ninth Conversation**
A Global Effect .......................................................... 101

**Helmut Schäfer – Invitation to the Dream**................ 111

**Roberto Ciulli – Biographical Data** ......................... 127

**The Theater an der Ruhr**......................................... 129

First Conversation

## Freedom in Prison

*Malgorzata Bartula*: How does one discover improvisation? Looking over your theatrical career as a whole – is it a particular experience, is it an insight? Can one do it when one is still only a twenty year-old or does one have to be older? Is it a question of how some one with a philosophical, categorising, determining mind has to exhaust himself in order to find his way through to a new country, to something that is unknown and uncertain?

*Roberto Ciulli*: First of all, I think one is making a mistake if one sees improvisation as something which only applies to theatre. Seen in this way, 'improvisation by actors' only means the actor has a certain freedom in putting a scene together in the first rehearsals. But improvisation has a lot more to do with life and with human beings than this. One can apply it in the theatre, but what improvisation is first of all is something that happens in life rather than a method specific to the theatre. Human beings improvise all the time. We are improvising now. From one sentence to the next.

*Malgorzata Bartula*: What am I going to hear that will surprise me?

*Roberto Ciulli*: And how will you react? Whether you now laugh or not. It is not possible for us to know what the next three minutes will bring. You know certain things, but the space for improvisation in one human being's day is immeasurably greater. Even if what you are doing is routine, and one might say you have no free space to improvise – precisely at that point you notice that improvisation is taking place here too. You do the same thing every morning, and yet it is not the same. You perform the same actions, but they are different. Even when a predetermined action is incredibly precise you will still improvise. And that is exactly what is interesting.

*Malgorzata Bartula*: Routine consists in the repetition of known sequences of actions.

*Roberto Ciulli*: Yes, you know that every morning begins with the same daily sequence, but at the core of this sequence you have a freedom which might change the quality of the everyday.

*Malgorzata Bartula*: One day I will put my coffee cup down two inches further away from me than I did before?

*Roberto Ciulli*: Improvisation does not mean altering the action. It could be like that, but that is not the decisive thing. It is what you feel about it that is different. It is not about changing the position of the cup; it is the quality of the feelings involved in such routine actions which changes.

*Malgorzata Bartula*: We are usually encouraged to reproduce known sequences of actions and arrangements. One might say that what is operating is a kind of dictate of the known, of routine repetition. And there is also an interdiction placed on the unknown. This is how this society maintains its sense of order. To that extent, what you are talking about is the moment of transgression.

*Roberto Ciulli*: It is a moment of freedom. As long as we cannot break out of certain actions we are imprisoned. Even in the most minimal space we are in a prison. And improvisation does not mean changing prisons. Catching the next flight to Tahiti is not improvisation, it is a breakout. Improvisation affects only the quality of feeling, the change that occurs in me during the daily repetition of the known. That is improvisation.

*Stefan Schroer*: What you are describing is a state of consciousness with regard to your own actions. Viewed in broader perspective that would imply not so much a changed way of life as a changed attitude to a life which does not change.

*Roberto Ciulli*: Yes, and a changed consciousness with regard to actions brings one in the positive case – I am talking about life, but there is a parallel with the theatre – to the discovery of freedom in prison. This is what makes the human being more aware and the quality of life in the given circumstances of the action greater. Thus, in life too, improvisation is a means to self-awareness, to the consciousness of the richness of the self. Improvisation is a way of becoming a human being who is aware of himself.

*Malgorzata Bartula*: The change of feeling, even during familiar actions which are repeated, a changed, intensive feeling will result in an action, an act. At some point it will also burst out of the prison.

*Roberto Ciulli*: That might be so. One achieves a sovereignty with regard to actions. Actions become less and less important, for one discovers that it is not the action which determines me, but I who determine the action. Then I can decide whether I want to burst out of the prison or not; but in any case I gain a greater sense of freedom. I think the most important thing about freedom, whether one is in prison or not, is the sense we have of it. In his *The Royal Game [Schachnovelle]*[1] Stefan Zweig describes the liberation of a person within an impossible situation. By improvising with the game of chess the person becomes the master of this situation. There is a difference whether you perform an act as master or you perform the same action as servant. Improvisation describes only a subjective change in the world. In this connection it is not important whether someone breaks down the walls or not.

*Malgorzata Bartula*: Has your career been that of a playmaker with the emphasis on the maker? Has improvisation in the sense in which you describe it become more important over time? Did you start doing it with actors when you realised how unimportant the making is?

*Roberto Ciulli*: Yes. The plot is interchangeable. That is the nice thing about being an actor, that is the nice thing about acting. Even if one needs it, the plot is completely interchangeable, the feeling is not. That is why when I work in the theatre I no longer focus on plot.

---

[1] Stefan Zweig's *Schachnovelle*, first published in 1941, was translated into English as *The Royal Game* by B.W. Huebsch and published in 1944.

I think it is stupid to direct plots, and actors who simply act out plots are just as stupid. But you have to have one, i.e., you need some kind of framework. A theatrical production is a prison, really. You have to create this marked out space. But theatre has the advantage over life that you can throw out the plots again, that is the nice thing. Nevertheless, there are directors who drill actors to focus on a plot like circus trainers and do not take the freedom to throw their ideas away. In the end, the aim is not to throw plots away again and again, that would be just as stupid. It is to understand that they are interchangeable. Then you can decide in favour of one plot and try to get to grips with it. And you can try to seize the enormous wealth of freedom in it, to repeat the same gesture which, however, is always different, dissimilar.

*Malgorzata Bartula*: Did you begin improvising in the theatre from the very beginning? How did you improvise in *Il Globo*?[2] Or didn't you do so? When was the first time?

*Roberto Ciulli*: I can't say. From my childhood I was always very much on my own. I think people, particularly children who are very lonely, have this experience. And I got to that point very early. Then I lost it.

*Malgorzata Bartula*: The experience of the prison?

*Roberto Ciulli*: The awareness of being in a prison. Your freedom of action is very restricted, you are lonely, you have no one to talk to, you have no one. And now, it is as it is in *The Royal Game*. This person is alone, he has to consider what he should do so that he does not go under. He starts playing chess like a child playing with toy soldiers for the first time. But then comes the next stage. They notice that you are enjoying this game and they take your toy soldiers away from you. Then you haven't got any toy soldiers any

---

[2] *Il Globo* was a theatre founded by Roberto Ciulli in Milan in 1960 and run by him until 1962. It performed in a marquee and concentrated its activities in the outer suburbs of the city.

more. And so now you begin to imagine them in your mind. You tell yourself, I can manage this way too. They have punished me and taken my toy soldiers away, but I'll go on playing anyway. That's what the person in the *The Royal Game* does. He makes chess pieces out of bread and when he is discovered they take them away from him too. So he starts playing chess in his head. And I think children who are lonely very soon learn this possibility of freedom. I could never play with other children, I was only ever in our house. I was only ever allowed to go as far as the garden gate, where the street children were. I showed off my expensive toys to attract the other children's attention so that they would play with me. And they would play with this idiot because they could steal his toys. When my mother saw what was going on, I wasn't even allowed to go to the garden gate any more. I was only ever in the company of older people where there weren't any other children. I was not allowed to speak either. That was forbidden. I could not say: Mum, I am thirsty. The only thing I could do was try to attract my mother's eye and then give her a secret signal. But I was not allowed to speak.

*Malgorzata Bartula*: Except when you were presented as a clown, though?

*Roberto Ciulli*: Presented yes, but that is something else. That was a lot later, I was not a child then.

*Malgorzata Bartula*: But how can a person confined in this kind of isolation, in this kind of loneliness and imprisonment ever meet anyone else? Is such a meeting possible at all?

*Roberto Ciulli*: First of all, let me say something about improvising on one's own. If an actor or someone has not understood that improvisation is a subjective feeling, he will not be able to improvise with anyone else either. Without improvising with one's self actors will only vary actions, they will not improvise.

*Stefan Schroer*: So the way to a successful encounter where actors really do begin to improvise with one another is not so much an acting process as a human one?

*Roberto Ciulli*: Certainly. If the actor is not a human being, he is only an ass. That's it. On the other hand, there are actors who possess this knowledge, as human beings, and then they will be actors as well. With most so-called actors this is not the case, though. On the contrary, there are many who have never had the opportunity to see that they could be actors. They went other ways. And then, in life, the talent of improvising is lost.

*Malgorzata Bartula*: Georges Bataille says that a human being derives his awareness of being a human being from observing prohibitions. His sovereign dignity, on the other hand, he gains from transgressing interdictions. From the way you have described your development as a director, you began as a playmaker with a philosophical approach. With the idea that you could determine out of your own head what a world picture taking the form of a theatrical production would look like. To that extent you sought to create a particular world.

*Roberto Ciulli*: I did once describe it like that, as one possible explanation. In reality there is more to it. I do not know what it was that attracted me to the theatre, but I do know that I began with a very great deal of modesty, with the greatest respect for the theatre and for actors. I do not know where I got that from. At university I was very successful, in my second year I was already taking part in conferences and writing philosophical articles. I was headed for an academic career. I could have had a university chair at home and I would have been the youngest professor at an Italian university in the fifties.

*Malgorzata Bartula*: And then Dionysos rang your door bell...

*Roberto Ciulli*: And I do not know why. Actually I was like a beggar when I began in the theatre, I had a sense of deference towards the theatre, theatre people, directors and actors. I have never really lost that. When I see a performance, as I did recently in Iran, and I realise that the director, in this case Bahram Beyzái, is truly a master, I feel like a beggar. And when I see a great actor on stage, I feel deep respect. And then, of course, I got caught up in the business of theatre, in this power game which is what the trivial world of the theatre is all about.

*Malgorzata Bartula*: But first of all, of course, in 1960 you set up your own theatre, *Il Globo*. How did you do that?

*Roberto Ciulli*: Well, yes, I did that with the nonchalance and the superficiality of a young man who simply said: this is what I'm going to do.

*Malgorzata Bartula*: ... and I'll call it right from the start *Il Globo*.

*Roberto Ciulli*: Yes. That will be *Il Globo* and I am going to do it. And I began to play the role of director.

*Malgorzata Bartula*: Did you want to become an actor?

*Roberto Ciulli*: Yes, I did actually want to be an actor, but they said I didn't have any talent, I shouldn't go on the stage under any circumstances. And I believed that.

*Malgorzata Bartula*: Who said that to you?

*Roberto Ciulli*: There was a theatre group at university, I had an audition there, and they said: "Forget it, you've got no talent at all." I believed them then. At the time people in Italy thought you couldn't be an actor if you hadn't studied at the Academy in Rome or at the *Piccolo Teatro*. Besides, I didn't speak the language of the Italian stage. I do in fact speak standard Italian, but the language of the theatre is different. It's a question of accent, "bene" and "bane", for instance. I say "bene". But in the theatre they say "bane". If you say "bene", you've had it. Then there was the fact that I was very shy and was quick to blush. I couldn't do anything about it. Auditioning on stage was a torment. So I said to myself, good, you are not going to be an actor. So directing it was.

*Malgorzata Bartula*: And so you discovered the role of director for yourself. I recently saw a tape of your 1990 production *Clowns* where you played the role of the circus director, Mr Loyal.

*Roberto Ciulli*: That was because the cast had been changed.

*Malgorzata Bartula*: But it lives from the fact that you imitate your erstwhile behaviour as a director and cannot become an actor.

✻

*Malgorzata Bartula*: When did you improvise for the first time in a sense that approximates to what you are doing now?

*Roberto Ciulli*: You mean in the theatre?

*Malgorzata Bartula*: Yes, of course – but we can go on talking about life if you prefer.

*Roberto Ciulli*: In the theatre very late. It was Gordana Kosanovic who taught me to understand all that correctly.[3]

*Malgorzata Bartula*: Had you already got to know her before the Horváth Project in Berlin in 1979?

*Roberto Ciulli*: That was afterwards. We were already improvising in the Horváth Project though. The project was rather unusual compared to the theatre of the day, but it was not improvisation on the level we are talking about. I only came to understand that through my work with Gordana.

*Malgorzata Bartula*: Was she already aware of that?

*Roberto Ciulli*: She was.

*Malgorzata Bartula*: Could she work like that? Or was she not able to work like that although she knew that one ought to work that way?

*Roberto Ciulli*: No, no, for her it was all a matter of course. She was still young, but she had all that in her. She knew that in the sense that I knew it too, but she knew it as an actress too. She was the sort of person who became an actor, I was the sort of person who did not become an actor. That is why I was able to understand

---

[3] Gordana Kosanovic, born in 1953 in Valjevo, Yugoslavia. Trained as an actor with Prof. Ognjenka Milcevic at the Faculty for Dramatic Art in Belgrade. As an actress in theatre and film Gordana Kosanovic was one of the best known and respected artists in Yugoslavia. After working with Roberto Ciulli and Helmut Schäfer in the *Decameron* at the Atelje 212 (Belgrade) she became a founder member of the *Theater an der Ruhr*, where until 1986 she appeared in twelve productions, among them as Lulu in Wedekind's *Lulu*, as Puck in Shakespeare's *A Midsummer Night's Dream*, as Electra in Sophocles' *Electra*, as Nina in Chekhov's *Seagull* and as Karoline in Horvath's *Kasimir and Karoline*. Gordana Kosanovic died in Belgrade in 1986. Her life and her work as an artist are the subject of the memorial volume *Gordana Kosanovic 1953-1986*, published by the *Theater an der Ruhr*.

her. I can say that in the years from '79 to '86, until her death, I came to understand what acting was all about. Everything I know today. It was through her.

*Malgorzata Bartula*: Was Gordana Kosanovic's central idea what she formulated in her notes as an appeal to human beings: "Who has forbidden you to be heroes?"

*Roberto Ciulli*: In relation to one's own actions and one's consciousness of freedom, it was precisely that.

*Malgorzata Bartula*: She says that contradictoriness is part of being a hero. Did you found the *Theater an der Ruhr*[4] as a result of the kind of clarity which was emerging through working with Gordana Kosanovic?

*Roberto Ciulli*: No, the idea of founding the theatre was older than that.

*Malgorzata Bartula*: I want to ask you whether when you set up the theatre you were already aware that this theatre should also be established as a place where improvisation could take place in the sense you have described?

*Roberto Ciulli*: Many other factors come into play when one is setting up a theatre. And even after you have done so it is still a struggle. Even at the time Gordana was here there were massive confrontations with other actors. There is always a struggle between people who have understood something and desire it and people who have understood nothing at all and who are thus not in a position to desire it, who desire something different. This struggle is a constant one in the theatre, and only a few people ever succeed in moving things in the right direction. But, as in life, we never manage to achieve everything. Never.

*Malgorzata Bartula*: The first group is always in the minority.

---

[4] Throughout this volume we are retaining the German name of the theatre, *Theater an der Ruhr*, whose English translation would be Theatre on the Ruhr. The Ruhr is, of course, the name of the river which flows through Mülheim and which gave its name to the famous industrial area. We are likewise retaining the German name *Junges Theater* for the more recently founded Youth Theatre.

*Roberto Ciulli*: Yes. And it is mostly the women who dare to move a long way forward. And either they do it in a way others understand, or the others do not understand them and then there is a struggle. This is repeated over and over again, because you can't force anyone to do something he does not understand. If he does not understand it for his own part, there is no sense in it.

*Malgorzata Bartula*: If he has no insight...

*Roberto Ciulli*: Yes, real understanding is an insight. If he does not have that in his body, there is no sense in it. One can then try and help him. But if – for extraneous reasons such as vanity, hunger for power ...

*Malgorzata Bartula*: Anxiety...

*Roberto Ciulli*: ... yes, anxiety too – he refuses to take such a step, then a conflict begins. And if he starts to pull in another direction as well, you will recognise sooner or later that one can't work together any more. And then there has to be a separation.

*Malgorzata Bartula*: The visible world, which is in the majority, struggles against the minority of the invisible world.

*Roberto Ciulli*: Yes. The majority has a notion of acting which has to do with making an external effect. Only very few have the correct insight.

*Malgorzata Bartula*: In general what dominates is the perfecting of externalization.

*Roberto Ciulli*: Yes, actors believe they are succeeding through a communication, which is empty at the core. Here lies the great misunderstanding with regard to the audience. Genuine communication takes place when an actor reaches someone subjectively, really affects him. What we usually have in the theatre, however, is a superficial kind of communication which only appears to reach many people.

***

*Malgorzata Bartula*: If you want to realise this utopia you have been describing you first have to free people from the pressure to achieve a result which is oriented to externals. You have to arouse in them a trust in what is not superficial, in what is communicated in another way. Besides running the whole operation and keeping a forty-man ensemble together for twenty years, your work has, therefore, consisted mainly in demonstrating to the people you work with the necessity of taking responsibility themselves for their own artistic expression.

*Roberto Ciulli*: I cannot imagine doing anything other than trying to transform people into characters. That is the reason why I make theatre. And I succeed in doing that best when the people who work here, particularly the actors of course, are prepared to trust me a lot. When I sense this trust then I become much freer myself. It is most difficult when people – for whatever reason – do not open themselves to me. The difficulty with this lies in the fact that I am not looking for blind trust. I am not interested in playing the role of a guru, but in how consciously a person working with me is prepared to go along the path of trust. Consciously, not through depending on me.

*Stefan Schroer*: The role of the guru excludes a relationship based on mutual trust at the level of ideas. If it is a question of preserving the freedom of whoever is working with you, this is not going to work by trusting in a guru but only through something like trust based on friendship or love.

*Roberto Ciulli*: And finally of course it is a matter of the trust one bears in oneself. And through the constellation it provides, through what it opens up, the theatre is really the only place where it is possible to go down such a path. But even in theatre I cannot simply exchange people after a while if I notice we're not getting across to one another. Even then we are still forced to go on working together. That is what makes it difficult, and one notices it through the differences in acting which one is not aware of from the outside, but which for me are very painful. There are performances I cannot bear to watch. I force myself to watch them because it is my job to criticise every evening, but for me it is terribly difficult to see in a performance someone who has missed his opportunity and whom I cannot put on the right track any more. The play goes on, but his chance is lost, it is dead.

*Malgorzata Bartula*: The balance between a humanist and a guru is very difficult to strike, because we have been brought up to imitate the categories of others, and since we are no longer sure of ourselves and do not trust ourselves, we look to other authorities. In our weak moments, in our uncertainty we always look to figures who show us how to do something.

*Roberto Ciulli*: Nevertheless, there is something important in what you are saying. If you have met a person you think has a positive effect on you, then I think it is right to follow him. Not blindly, but in the awareness that this person is telling me something. I don't exactly know what this is, but I can feel it, I want to help him put what he is trying to do into practice, I have confidence in him. I think such willingness and capability is important in order to be like that to someone in whom others have confidence. And then one leaves this person. That is the difference between the so-called master and the guru and other such dreadful figures. In my youth, for instance, I twice had the opportunity to develop such a relationship. One of them was with my father, the other with my professor. The latter was a master, and I really loved him. I felt that I must go to him and that he needed me too. He helped me to become someone like that too. And if I were to meet someone today, who can communicate that to me again, I would follow that person. I have not met such a person or I have passed them by without realising it, but I would follow this path in order to reach something new. And vice versa, I hope that people who approach me know exactly why they are doing so.

*Malgorzata Bartula*: If you had not attracted people, however, you would not perhaps have begun what you have created.

*Roberto Ciulli*: Most probably yes. That's perhaps part of it. Certain people do have this power to attract others and thus acquire responsibility, and then the question is what they make of it. It does happen to me that actors or other people feel attracted to me and they come to me – and then they have nothing in common with me. A year later I know it was all a misunderstanding.

*Stefan Schroer*: You wanted to be the one to set a process of self-emancipation in motion and what happened was quite the opposite, what takes place is subjection?

*Roberto Ciulli*: Either subjection or there is a power struggle.

*Malgorzata Bartula*: If one were to set about defining a master, would a master be an improviser who knows how to maintain the balance between a strong sense of self and an encounter with another? That would make improvisation an encounter of two masters, so to speak.

*Roberto Ciulli*: I think that any person who manages to gain freedom inside the prison and knows how to build on it, is a master.

*Malgorzata Bartula*: Those are the heroes.

*Roberto Ciulli*: Yes, precisely, those are the heroes.

*Malgorzata Bartula*: The term is justified; we are not talking about Heracles.

*Roberto Ciulli*: Exactly. In the Camargue there lived an old man, about seventy years old, a strange chap. He was not an intellectual, he kept horses, and he was a fisherman. I recall a scene which was actually quite brutal. It was shortly before the foundation of the *Theater an der Ruhr*. I was in the Camargue with Helmut[5] and Habben.[6] Habben knew this man and we went to visit him. There was a girl there, she must have been about nineteen. That evening we were invited to dinner, and the girl spent the whole time crying.

---

[5] Helmut Schäfer, born in Cologne in 1952, studied philosophy, sociology, art history and literature at the Universities of Frankfurt, Heidelberg and San Diego. He then taught at various institutions in Amsterdam, Cologne, Frankfurt and Berlin. Since 1972 he has worked in the theatre, particularly as literary adviser. Helmut Schäfer is co-founder and, together with Roberto Ciulli and Gralf-Edzard Habben, one of the artistic directors of the *Theater an der Ruhr*.

[6] Gralf-Edzard Habben was born in Moers in 1934. He trained at the School of Industrial Design in Krefeld. He has worked as stage designer at a number of theatres, in association for instance with Pina Bausch, Kai Brarak, Roberto Ciulli, Ever Diamantstein, Günther Fleckenstein, Hansgünther Heyme, Jörg Hube, Kurt Hübner, Valentin Jeker, Hans Lietzau, Claus Peymann, and Dieter Reibke. Gralf-Edzard Habben is co-founder and, together with Roberto Ciulli and Helmut Schäfer, one of the artistic directors of the *Theater an der Ruhr*.

We did not know why. It was embarrassing. But he behaved perfectly naturally, as though nothing was happening. In the end we asked him why she was crying. He answered: "She has to go away, tomorrow. She does not understand it, she is young. But she has to get away from me. It is over." I found that brutal, because the girl was obviously in love with the man. She was not his maid, she was a girl who had lived there with him for perhaps one or two months, and he thought she ought to leave now. I said: "I can't understand that." But then I did come to understand it. He was right. The girl wanted to stay with him until he died. But she had to get out, get away. That is a master. Even in solitude.

*Malgorzata Bartula*: In your work you aim to have a permanent company that is with you all the time.

*Roberto Ciulli*: Yes, but I have also said that I am proud and happy that I have got so many people away from the theatre. I do aim for a permanent company, but I would not have any difficulty understanding an actor who has reached a stage where it no longer suffices to be an actor and he would like to do something else. Being an actor is a stage in the journey of a person. One could die on stage, and then one would have to ask oneself whether that constitutes the greatest happiness. I am not so sure that it is. Molière is someone who got caught up in the plots. Perhaps being an actor is simply an extraordinary opportunity to achieve something else. And that is where for me one of the tasks of theatre lies. Either die, or move on to something else. Gordana died. What she would have done I have no idea.

*Malgorzata Bartula*: I certainly believe that you are able to separate from an actor who has reached a certain point. But this is a utopian case, a notional one.

*Roberto Ciulli*: It has certainly never happened to me.

*Malgorzata Bartula*: You see.

*Roberto Ciulli*: Perhaps it will happen to me sometime.

※

*Malgorzata Bartula*: The history of the twenty years of the *Theater an der Ruhr* is the history of the liberation of man from the domination of an understanding that seeks to categorise. It is also a history of how man liberates himself from time, although people do constantly leave in an unfinished state, and that repeatedly.

*Roberto Ciulli*: Yes, it is a workshop. In the old sense of craft, too. I always resist the usual term "the craft of acting". There isn't one which is valid for all. The craft consists in an actor finding his own means of expression, for himself, for what is in him. It is completely absurd to maintain one is developing a universally valid craft for actors. One can work at it to a certain extent, but the proper way is that each actor has to find his own craft. And not one which is said to be a craft for all. For example, in recent years Simone Thoma[7] has taken this path, slowly. Someone else's craft isn't any use to her because no other means are of any use to her for what she has in her; she has to find her own craft as an actress. That is my job, and the happy moments for me are when I can see it emerging. This craft the actor has found contains the greatest possibility for real communication. The audience does not see the craft, but they do have the opportunity to recognise what is behind the craft. They receive the message about what this person is. Craft is only the means of expressing something that has to come out, that is within. I want to differentiate that. Many actors exercise a craft, but only because of a bad conscience, because at heart they would really like to be craftsmen. They are afraid of art. But Michelangelo's greatness does not lie in his craft. His craft is at the service of something else. And that is true of actors, too. Crafts can be learnt, but what is at stake is what is behind it and only one's own craft can assist that in emerging, in being expressed. In this sense Michelangelo has his craft and Goya has his. In art there is no craft which can be valid for all.

---

[7] Simone Thoma, born in 1966, studied acting in Freiburg and Hamburg and has been acting at the *Theater an der Ruhr* since 1993.

SECOND CONVERSATION

# The Age of Apes

*Malgorzata Bartula*: You directed *Ein Bericht für eine Akademie* [*A Report for an Academy*][1] and you cast Ferhade Feqi in the role of the ape.[2] Here I see an actor imprisoned in a glass cage, which serves as his dressing room, but at the same time I see a foreigner exposed to the highly literary language of Franz Kafka. A line in the text impressed me: "I did not want freedom, only a way out." The actor then emerges from the cage, he approaches the audience and fails to perform his act. There is no trained flea, the classic clown number does not work. And in the *Schachnovelle* [*The Royal Game*] the person who has gained his freedom in his mind goes insane.

*Roberto Ciulli*: No, he doesn't. On the voyage to South America he meets the world chess champion and almost wins.

*Stefan Schroer*: The episode you have been talking about happened in SS detention, in solitary. It is just before he is going to have to make his statement and he saves himself by improvising with the game of chess. That works for a time but the inner freedom this person has gained through the imagination makes him become more and more demented. He is forced to split himself in two. He plays against himself and at the end he does in fact go insane for a short time. You were talking about freedom of choice: I can blow the

---

[1] In the production of Franz Kafka's *Bericht für eine Akademie* [*A Report for an Academy*], which had its première in March 1998, the ape Rotpeter [Red Peter] is a vaudeville artist who is in a glass dressing room preparing to go on and is telling the story of his assimilation while doing so. After the end of his report he performs the classic number for clowns in which a trained flea refuses to do a fancy dive from a springboard.

[2] Ferhade Feqi, born in Bingöl (Turkish Kurdistan) in 1967, has been acting with the *Theater an der Ruhr* since 1992.

place up or not, that depends on what I decide. But in the *The Royal Game*, and somewhat differently in Kafka's *Report* – this is the central theme of your production, too – this absolute freedom to make one's own decision is not available.

*Roberto Ciulli*: If one says that the logical step is to blow up the prison, that is a step a human being takes into the world, a step which lies within his freedom of choice. The step to blow the place up, to act, to change is a step from an inner freedom to a transformative act, a step for example towards terrorism. I would not say that this is a law. I am only saying that the first step is necessary in order to attain what is possible for us without seeking escape in religion or ideology. It is a question of finding oneself as an individual.

*Stefan Schroer*: But the interesting thing about the motif of *The Royal Game* is the active element, the destructive nature of the prison. If that element were to remain passive, the human being really would have freedom of choice: am I satisfied with what I have, or do I want more, or something different? But since his situation in prison continues to have a destructive effect, it cannot be maintained. He has no freedom of choice. His inner freedom ends in insanity. That describes the impossibility of living a correct life within the wrong one.

*Malgorzata Bartula*: Ulrike Meinhof wrote from death row on the eighth floor of Stammheim prison that it is the lack of a person to communicate with that brings about self-destruction. The way death row was arranged was perfect for that, with its blank walls which you are not allowed to hang anything on, completely sound-proofed so that no noise can be heard. Where no opposition is possible, we have self-destruction, self-destruction for lack of a person to deal with.

*Roberto Ciulli*: I brought up the *The Royal Game* since it raises the question of how one survives in such a case. It is an example of an extreme situation, and we were talking about life, about the freedom we have, every morning, in the course of the same action in a prison which always remains the same. Heiner Müller said: "I stand in front of the mirror in the morning and I say, I don't know this person, I am not going to wash his face." That is the inner freedom, that is the change. Every day I do the same thing, but I say: I am not going to wash him. It is a question of the feeling involved and not of an action.

*Stefan Schroer*: Taking this theme a little further, I wonder whether inner freedom does not presuppose the freedom of a society which actually exists.

*Roberto Ciulli*: Good, but it's a question of the small step by which one assists people in extreme situations to gain the experience and understanding which will help them to survive. It is a question of not simply allowing oneself apathetically to be oppressed by life but of becoming aware not only of one's lack of freedom but also of one's inner freedom – that is what will enable one to change and to survive. That is what we are doing, that is life. What we are doing is really only that.

*Roberto Ciulli*: We are now moving into a phase where we can allow ourselves to make a radical break. To remind ourselves of why we are making theatre, to remind ourselves that this place can't simply be exchanged for some other. And I say that the age of apes is coming. Taking that as our theme is important now. That is the reason why I wanted to put on something like this with someone who was not a recognised actor and who in terms of the categories of the German theatre wouldn't normally be allowed to go on stage and speak. I wanted to do it specifically with a person like this who has his particular biography and who is the very incarnation of the contradiction or, if you like, the bad conscience of doing what he is and not being allowed to. This is what makes the evening very political. Its provocative effect lies in the fact that it is precisely this person who is speaking Kafka's text. German theatres have appropriated this sacred text as an opportunity for brilliant performances by actors who are showered with praise for reciting classical German literature wearing the guise of an ape. That is what the tradition is here. The text was written by a Jew, who spoke German and if he had lived any longer, he would have landed in

Auschwitz. And now I come up with a person who isn't a venerable actor at some subsidised municipal theatre but an immigrant who has never even been near a theatre school.

*Stefan Schroer*: It is not about theatre, but about life.

*Roberto Ciulli*: And something remarkable happens. It is the audience who are sitting there in prison. Not the actor. He is content. And at the end the audience cannot bear being forced into the role of those booing[3] – that's too irritating for words. When the actor approaches the audience, it is over. If as a member of the audience I think I am not one of them, then I laugh about it. But if all of a sudden I feel that I am part of the leisure society we have here, then I obviously have a problem.

*Malgorzata Bartula*: Then I applaud out of embarrassment. – This *Report* is the story of an ape, to stay with the image, who knows how to act like a human being. Knowing that freedom is impossible since death makes it so, what each one of us has described for us in your show, whether he's a Jew in Prague or you here or I myself, is an escape route, which lies in the playing, in the very fact of being an actor. Wearing a well-looked after fur underneath and mastering the rules of the game on the outside.

*Roberto Ciulli*: But what Ferhade Feqi performs is the story of total assimilation. This ape is not an actor in our sense of the word. The only chance for someone like him to enter society lies in playing the scapegoat. Our society exploits outsiders. The story is a negative one. It shows us a human being who is considering his options and who is suffering, since his only chance lies in assimilating, in becoming our scapegoat.

*Stefan Schroer*: In the end he is the scapegoat. But when he performs he is applauded.

*Roberto Ciulli*: No he isn't.

---

[3] During the vaudeville performance in this production a sound recording is played of an audience whose applause is gradually transformed into boos which get louder and louder as they watch the failure of the number with the flea. At which point Red Peter attacks the real audience with a club. After he has displayed his scar he leaves the stage, looking back at the audience as he does so.

*Stefan Schroer*: He says he is a recognised vaudeville artist.

*Roberto Ciulli*: Turn on the television and watch American wrestlers entering the ring and people screaming: "Boo! Finish him off!" That is the success they have. They are recognised when people scream: "Kill him!"

*Malgorzata Bartula*: It's a story of failure. The failure of someone who has assimilated, at the very moment of success.

*Roberto Ciulli*: A necessary act which this racist society needs in order to come to terms with such a person. It only accepts losers. It's an evil sport. People come to see it in their thousands. And they do scream. It is an anti-story. You do not achieve any recognition as a human being, your success consists in appearing as a scapegoat, as an ape. His failure is not a sudden defeat, but it is part of his act. It happens every evening, it is always the same. The club he attacks the audience with is a prop. It's not something that suddenly comes over him. This could be repeated endlessly. The same every evening. But what happens when he leaves the stage? He looks back at the audience and in this look I see that his person has been wounded. That is no longer part of the role, it's personal. Cocain will help him to bear it. But the wound remains there in the human being.

*Malgorzata Bartula*: The very fact of making theatre implies *a priori* that you are optimistic, even when the blackest story is being told. What brand of optimism do you inscribe over your proscenium arch? I know, in your theatre there isn't an arch. Perhaps because you are not an optimist? But the curtain rises. I would have liked to see the actor march off with more pride, less broken.

*Roberto Ciulli*: He shows beforehand what options he has, what creativity. He reveals a trace of it. He is a human being. He shows how he deals with this text. Associations are awakened with this image. But in society he has no chance. It's either prison or vaudeville theatre – so he opts for the vaudeville theatre.

*Stefan Schroer*: And the positive aspect of the arch is: the ape's look is the one, and that of Ferhade Feqi would be the proud one.

*Roberto Ciulli*: The positive thing is the recognition of what should be done. Am I free, am I prepared to listen to this text from such a person? Yet in myself I can feel resistance. That can be a great gain. This evening in the theatre makes clear to me that I am not tolerant. We have not yet got that far. Recognising that is what this *Report* gives me. I understand that for the audience this is a difficult evening in the theatre, even I felt some resistance to it. But we are not making theatre in order to consolidate the *status quo* in society.

*Malgorzata Bartula*: In the novel *America* there is the Oklahoma nature theatre. Come hither all of you, you are all needed, no special abilities are required, all of you are actors here. Walter Benjamin says, all Kafka's characters are theatrical characters. And if there is an escape, then it consists in being an actor in life. On the outside a character, on the inside the fur. I understood the failure like this: as soon as a person allows himself to reveal the fur, like a clown who displays his sadness, he is lost.

*Roberto Ciulli*: Yes. But it actually began in a different way. This act is all he has. He became a cruel, evil, violent trainer only gradually. In our terms the act was poor, but the audience needs greater and greater aggressions. He has no other chance.

*Stefan Schroer*: But with his melancholy look at the end he asserts something of his own. The wrestlers depart shouting and cursing. There aren't any sad looks there. It's the same with the clown. The utopian moment thus becomes visible on the stage.

*Roberto Ciulli*: Yes, because we are in the theatre, not watching wrestling. The audience has to understand that, but it must do something against it too. For actually that is a real moment. In 1979 we did *Cyclops*. At the end of the performance, everyone leaves, only the cyclop, Manuela Alfons,[4] remains behind, dazzled. This lasted five minutes. We did it almost a hundred times and twice it

---

[4]  Manuela Alfons, born 1946, trained as an actor in Bochum, worked with Roberto Ciulli in Göttingen, Cologne and Düsseldorf in the years 1967-1981.

happened that a member of the audience got up, went up to the cyclop and embraced him. Now we are doing *A Report for an Academy* – no one has come to the performance who would have reacted like that. The audience did not enter into the play. They were not up to their role.

*Malgorzata Bartula*: Was it planned for the actor to improvise? According to whether the audience was prepared to take on its role? Was that agreed in advance?

*Roberto Ciulli*: No. But I did count on the real audience saying "No" as he went off, and then approaching him.

*Stefan Schroer*: What direction would a reaction have taken? In the case of the cyclop you described it as compassionate rather than liberating...

*Roberto Ciulli*: No, not like that. Even as he is going off, the reaction should begin, someone should hold him back and not simply sit there to wait for the end. That's where humanity begins.

*Stefan Schroer*: Not simply regarding themselves as an audience which has been taped.

*Roberto Ciulli*: Yes. But in a world where you can make money or produce entertainment with that type of failure there was no chance of that.

*Stefan Schroer*: But earlier you described the positive moment, which one might also call utopian, as the recognition of the negative. The negativity, that the only possibility of an escape lies in the process of total assimilation or adaptation, allows us, if so clearly felt, to recognise the countervailing positive element. That is the only possibility. Formulating a positive utopia is kitsch, but making it possible to experience failure in this way and the very act that it is possible – keyword: arch – to fail in this way is an unexpressed utopia, an unexpressed humanity.

*Roberto Ciulli*: It doesn't matter what form one decides in favour of, I wouldn't always want to call other forms kitsch, we have to recognise that this is what our work is. We have to advance considerably beyond actual reality. That is our fundamental work.

Actors must become more aware of this. This play, the atmosphere, the whole process of changing society, the leisure culture: on no account must we be satisfied with the mere description of conditions as they are.

*Roberto Ciulli*: What this *Report* tells us about is also my own story. In order to function you have to cut off part of your soul. If you move from one culture to another, you always cut off part of your own culture. Either you are lucky and you find your way back to this part of your soul somehow, some time. Then it's fine. Or you are condemned to living for all time deprived of a part of you. That is where this sadness comes from, the bad conscience. Recently a member of the audience came up and spoke to me after a performance. He thought *Pinocchio Faust*[5] was very good. He could not forget it, but he was not so enthusiastic about *Bericht*. And then this successful businessman working in industry told me that when he was ten years old, he had wanted to be a singer. And he did sing, with an orchestra. But then he came to Germany and he could not do so any longer. The two things just did not go together. But now, he told me, partly because of our theatre, he was going to organise a concert in Tashkent. So I asked him: "Are you aware that what you are telling me is what you have just seen on the stage?" This person, too, had given up part of his soul. You are in the theatre and what you see is yourself. It is difficult to be a member of an audience. Just as difficult as being an actor. Perhaps even more difficult.

---

[5] *Pinocchio Faust* (première in October 1997) is the first part of the *Faust Project* developed by the *Theater an der Ruhr* within the framework of the *Silk Road Project* (see Note 19). Carlo Collodi's fairy tale *Pinocchio* is prefaced as a fiction of childhood to the tragedy of the scholar which takes up Part 1 of Goethe's *Faust*, in which Faust, doubting life and thought, is tempted by Mephisto to begin a new life. While the *Faust* production sticks closely to Goethe's text, the action and the text of the *Pinocchio* story are reinvented in the form of improvisations by the actors.

*Malgorzata Bartula*: You wanted to give up the theatre once. But since then the flea has kept on jumping.

*Roberto Ciulli*: But there were times when I was the scapegoat.

*Malgorzata Bartula*: Your exits are always proud ones.

THIRD CONVERSATION

# A Better Prison

*Malgorzata Bartula*: The performances in your repertoire arose from a variety of production situations. *Teatro Comico*[1] emerged from a predetermined theme, albeit freely, while other performances arose from different circumstances. How would you describe an improvisation of this sort? How do you proceed when the theme is all you have?

*Roberto Ciulli*: First of all, *Teatro Comico* was the result of a normal decision in favour of a play, of two plays actually: *Impresario delle Smyrne* and *Teatro Comico*. Both these plays were written by Carlo Goldoni, and that determines the way they are usually played. *The Impresario of Smyrna* is familiar in Germany, too. Yet after rehearsing for four or five weeks we discovered that it would be much more sensible to free ourselves from the constraints of the text and to develop our own play. We asked ourselves once again: "What are we doing this play for?" And we found that we could not answer this question simply by doing a production of the Goldoni texts. So we decided to go for a radical new beginning. So we don't have a play, all we have is the title and the theme.

*Malgorzata Bartula*: Did the same thing happen with *The Servant of Two Masters* and with *Pinocchio*?

*Roberto Ciulli*: It was basically the same process. You take *The Servant of Two Masters* and if you believe that the leap into the

---

[1] In both *Teatro Comico* (premièred in November 1993) and *The Servant of Two Masters* (premièred in November 1994) the original texts by Carlo Goldoni were entirely replaced during the course of the rehearsals by improvised texts and new plot elements worked out by the actors. Only a few central motifs were retained from Goldoni.

present time is more important than the original text, then you retain the themes the play contains, you retain the basic situation, but you need a new text.

*Stefan Schroer*: In our first conversation you talked about the production and the text being a prison within which improvisation has to take place. You rejected the notion of improvisation being a way of inventing of plots and you emphasised that what is important is the feeling you have about yourself as an actor and your acting on stage. This raises the question as to whether there is more improvisation in *Faust* than in *Teatro Comico*?

*Roberto Ciulli*: No. The improvisations we do to find a play lead to the creation of a prison. The first thing the actors must do is construct a prison, whereas in *Faust* we already have one. What the actors perform in cases like *Teatro Comico* and *The Servant of Two Masters* are two types of improvisation. What the actor tries to do, or what we try to do in the pre-improvisation or the dramaturgical improvisation, is to construct this prison we have previously torn down before by rejecting Goldoni's original...

*Malgorzata Bartula*: ... a better prison.

*Roberto Ciulli*: Yes, and once we have a prison, either because we do not alter the text in any essential way, as for example with *Faust*, or because we have invented a new play, a new prison, that is when the second stage of the improvisation begins. This takes place in a very clearly marked framework, which has emerged collectively. One might ask: "where does a state come from, or a society? How do certain rules emerge?" That is the prison. And in terms of these rules, which in the case of *Teatro Comico* we made up and in that of *Faust* Goethe did, the quality lies in the unfolding of the individual creativity of each single person in the attempt to enliven this prison as far as possible. You always have this situation of having to create free spaces within the framework, within the given constraints so that individual creativity can unfold, a creativity which does not destroy everything, but which, on the contrary, enriches it. To this extent we have returned to my own origins. I wrote my doctorate on the relationship between the individual and the state, and this is really the theme I have been coming back to over and over ever since. For me there is a quite clear link from here to the theatre, and for this reason I believe that theatre should move closer to the centre of the consciousness of society. The ideal laboratory for working on the problems associated with the building of a society and for the social formations we have to invent so that a more humane society may emerge is the theatre. What we encounter there all the time is the dialectical relationship between the freedom of an individual and the order of a state, and the search for the maximum degree of freedom within a state, which is to say inside a prison.

*Malgorzata Bartula*: What kind of qualitative or practical difference is there between a concrete process of improvisation in the course of developing *Teatro Comico,* where the text is left behind, and that of Chekhov's *Cherry Orchard*? What does the work look like, how do you start?

*Roberto Ciulli*: In the case of *Teatro Comico* the actor has much greater freedom of movement. But this can be deceptive. The greater freedom he has is only an apparent one and this might lead him to believe that he is displaying greater creativity. Why? One can always question the given constraints, that is what makes improvisation easier here – if the actor is inventing the plot at the same time. With Chekhov it's more difficult, because the frame is given by someone you can't talk to. The framework is simply there. It might seem as though there is more creativity involved in the case of an invented play where the actor even makes up the texts, too. But the actor's creativity, the specific quality of the actor, does not lie in making up texts. For that reason Chekhov is a better yardstick with which to test the creativity of actors, for it is not necessarily true that those actors who find it easy to invent texts will be the better actors. That is a particular type of talent, but it does not tell us anything about the quality of an actor. On the other hand, if, for example, as in *Teatro Comico* a whole ensemble is working on the development of the text, what you get is a collective force, an erotic situation. There is competitiveness, so that even people who are normally quite reserved suddenly become confident and produce excellent texts. In rehearsal I never cease to be surprised at the way precise texts emerge from people who are not writers at all and at what potential there is in these people.

*Malgorzata Bartula*:  But how far can you go asking actors to invent texts? How much can an actor stand? Where are the limits of such improvisation? Once a process such as *Teatro Comico* is concluded and the première has taken place, the actors say: "Now we want to take a break, we aren't writers, we don't want to go on. The pressure is too great." So what is the quality of the relationship? Aren't you compensating for the actor making up the plot and the texts with his sensitivity as an actor?

*Roberto Ciulli*: I beg you, let's not start talking about the pressure of invention. How would a writer describe the pressure on him? And yet you are right on one point: the actor's work does become more difficult because he cannot afford to take a break. The writer gets up from his desk if he does not feel like working any more, he goes for a walk or a ride on a motorbike. And sometime later he comes back. It's the same with painters and even composers. But the actor has a period of five hours, particularly in an institutional structure like this one where he is called upon to rehearse from 10 till 3 and then perform the same evening. He has to be creative all the time, if he is not creative, he is put under pressure. And there is a lot of pressure. That is what makes the difference, and so it's only natural that at some stage he will say no. The only thing he wants to do is simply to act. And yet I think the actor who has created his own texts – I am sure, we could test this out – won't any longer be aware that he did create them himself. In the meantime he will have gained some distance and when he acts he will do so as if some other author had written his texts. His status as author actually takes a different direction. That is the reason why I have separated the two processes – the inventing of a play and the improvisation. The actor has to find his lines anew as if they were by someone else, so that he can find them again. Although he put the text together himself, he has to find it so new each evening *as if* it were his own.

*Stefan Schroer*: You were talking about the relationship between the state and the individual. Since then I have been thinking of *Pinocchio Faust*, where during rehearsals the two processes you described ran in parallel. In the *Pinocchio* section it was clear that the text corpus by Carolo Collodi was not the one being performed, and this is rather like the situation in *Teatro Comico*. What you have termed the apparently greater freedom and the apparently easier task of improvisation was to be observed there: it was effervescent and it took off in all sorts of unpredictable directions, but on a level where one knew that the actor would somehow bring out what had been previously determined. What one saw in the *Faust* section, on the other hand, was that somewhere up above there were figures from Goethe hovering about, and in order to remain in the picture the actor somehow had to raise himself up to their level. It was interesting to see how in the end a common level was in fact found. What we saw there was that Goethe's *Faust* is a despotic state, whereas the work on *Pinocchio* constitutes greater freedom, but also the greater task or challenge by a democracy or an anarchic state, where the whole structure has to be established as well and it is not simply a question of each individual attempting to raise himself to the level of what already exists as an abstraction.

*Roberto Ciulli*: Good. But nevertheless I would still always want to defend Goethe.

*Stefan Schroer*: I didn't want to say anything against Goethe ...

*Roberto Ciulli*: Well, let's say defend in terms of this state. That is correctly observed, only I think there are literary texts, of which with all its faults *Faust* is one, which are carved in stone. To bring their language, their ideas to life is an enormous process, which is set in motion during rehearsals. Yet if you do something like we have with the *Faust* project, that is a task which will take a lifetime, which is never-ending. And I do not think, on the other hand, that working on *Pinocchio* is a lifetime's task in that sense. *Pinocchio* is what it is, and in ten or twenty years, another generation will be doing something different. But trying to awaken *Faust* to life, trying to turn it into a living performance, is a never-ending task. And it is the same if you take on Kleist or Büchner. In such cases the prison is even stronger, but nevertheless, if one views producing such texts as a process, the actor does have the opportunity to do them again each year and to do them differently. It is then that a work by such a merciless genius of an author is an incredible gift.

*Stefan Schroer*: As an actor it would probably be impossible to create a figure like Faust out of one's own resources. But nor can he simply take Goethe's text and act it. I've seen that happen often enough in other theatres, particularly with *Faust*. The challenge is to project oneself into this character. By contrast, the *Pinocchio* material was at the level of children's literature, although it was based on good idea. And it was precisely the actor's task to make this idea his own and to express it while at the same time going beyond the original literary text.

*Roberto Ciulli*: The difference is that the *Pinocchio* material is the richer, the greater the personal input of the actors. It becomes more profound the more the ensemble of actors is able to function at a personal level. In a scene that is recreated in each new performance. Only in *Faust* you don't get very far by being personal. The dimensions are quite different.

*Stefan Schroer*: Where is the improvisation to be found in the process of bringing *Faust* to life?

*Roberto Ciulli*: The improvisation is reduced to zero. There is always this feeling of the actor facing a blank wall. Which is to say the actor is constantly faced with the impossible. There is no fulfilment. One always goes ever deeper, ever further. Then one acts in a performance for three years or so, and suddenly one says to oneself: What on earth have I been acting up to now? This evening, I have finally got it. That is the kind of process one would wish all artists to go through. How many attempts does one go through before an image is successfully caught? How many sketches? Or how many false trails are there behind a literary work or a composition? And such attempts are made by the actor every evening. The type of actor I mean. That is improvisation.

*Stefan Schroer*: In this case you are referring to the actor during the performance too?

*Roberto Ciulli*: Yes, certainly. An actor who has understood that he is only improvising will also understand that he is also improvising when he is playing Goethe. But he will understand it in the same sense as an artist does who has a dream in his head and until he reaches the point where he can paint the smile he has in his head he has a Sisyphean task before him. That is what the actor does every evening. In the performance as well. There is no division.

*Stefan Schroer*: You have also spoken about some performances which you cannot bear to watch, certain moments in the work of an actor who has had his chance and now can no longer be helped. The chance he has had of attaining this knowledge has passed, and for this reason he can no longer develop his life on the stage since improvisation is no longer possible.

*Roberto Ciulli*: But if you see what an actor is trying to do in the performances and you say to him: "I have understood what you are doing, I think your way of working on the character is right" – then the director can still be effective as a midwife in the performances, too. But there aren't many actors who do that. That is why watching performances, exercising this form of control, is such a torment for directors. Because one can see right away whether an actor is progressing or not. And if he is not progressing, there is nothing you can do about it. I cannot explain to someone why he is not in love. That can't be done. Nevertheless we do carry out our work here very seriously. I am one of the few directors who watch their own performances very frequently. There are cases where I really do not want to do this because I know from the start that it will be pointless.

*Stefan Schroer*: But isn't it also the possible that you will gain a lot of pleasure from seeing progress taking place?

*Roberto Ciulli*: Yes, of course there is, if that happens. But here we are talking about very long periods of time, about something which only develops over time. There are actors who give me very great pleasure. That is clear, and that is the finest moment: there are people who suddenly blossom forth.

*Malgorzata Bartula*: That has to do with infatuation. Theatre is a luxury to the extent that one is coming together for the sake of an idea as part of a collective whose members derive great pleasure from being with one another. On your own it is much more difficult, and that is precisely what happens in life.

*Roberto Ciulli*: Yes, Unfortunately, however, there are so many categories, or people too, who prevent precisely that. It is difficult enough in life. You live with a man and you have children, you live as a family, and then suddenly a child who has not said a word so far blossoms. That causes great pleasure for the whole family. Everybody is enthralled, everyone suddenly feels motivated. In the theatre, as a rule, it is the other way round. In a structure like that of the theatre what happens is often the opposite. The structures of the theatre are power structures, they are determined by competition, and that is why such phenomena cause such great difficulties. One never manages to sort it out. We have that in our theatre too, but we have tried to deal with it. I have myself experienced how a particular person blossoming has stimulated everyone, has had a positive effect on everyone. One experiences with others what one has not experienced with oneself. Not yet. One sees that something like this is possible. When one person develops his creativity it should actually always have a positive effect on others, not the other way round. Since it is a challenge and also a confirmation: if an ape like him can do this, I can too.

*Malgorzata Bartula*: Would that be an answer to the question: where does the director improvise?

*Roberto Ciulli*: Directors are responsible for a product, which is short-lived. That's why a director is like a quick lay. That is what this system is like. I am not one like that because I have decided to go in the other direction, to make long-term plans, to work with actors over periods of ten or fifteen years. I cannot separate from actors, it's rather they who separate from me. I never separate from actors. Because I always remain curious.

*Malgorzata Bartula*: What conditions have to be met before you can embark on an improvisation, before it can take place?

*Roberto Ciulli*: The first thing you have to do is recognise – instinctively, if you like – that the body thinks. That there is no distinction between mind and body. Otherwise you cannot improvise. Now we have to face the question I have always avoided: "is there a method of recognising that, of experiencing it?" I don't think there is. But nevertheless it is the prerequisite for an absolute trust in improvisation; what happens to you at a particular moment in time is what you go after. If body and mind are separated, there exists a dualism, a form of constant control, then you won't be able to improvise. There are many actors who only appear to be improvising, because their minds prevent them from doing so and the body cannot follow through on an idea.

*Malgorzata Bartula*: Isn't such control the first hurdle which always has to be surmounted? It is quite rare to meet someone who is not familiar with this division.

*Roberto Ciulli*: Yes, of course. You only meet such people. But there are those who have understood the problem and are working at it. I began doing improvisations about twenty years ago at a quite ordinary municipal theatre: you do an improvisation and the next day an actor comes up to you who has worked out everything he is going to improvise at home beforehand. So actors do think at home. And they even bring the props along with them for what they think they can improvise. These are ideas thought out in advance, and that is what one has to prevent.

*Malgorzata Bartula*: How?

*Roberto Ciulli*: By telling them that that is no good at all. I am not going to do it that way. Come back later. You are deceiving yourself if you try and take safety measures at home, because you know that the day after you'll be improvising. But it happens all the time, of course, and there is a quite banal reason for it. Even in rehearsals an actor wants to be successful, he wants to be sure of himself, in command of himself. What results from this is dramaturgical thinking. People cannot bear not being in command. But it is precisely when there is nothing there that the best situations are created. That is why I have to create trust and give people confidence. And what they experience is that at the very point where they know nothing at all, the whole thing takes on life.

*Stefan Schroer*: So if I imagine that in every moment of a rehearsal I'm going to be successful, I'm already barking up the wrong tree.

*Roberto Ciulli*: Yes. I have to trust in the place where I am as well as in who I am. To do that you have to have time – which is why the structures of the subsidised municipal theatres are all wrong. I can't develop trust in people I only spend six weeks with, because that reduces the whole thing to competition and to leadership. We need structures which enable the actor to develop his creativity.

*Roberto Ciulli*: The next condition is that you do not go into rehearsals every day thinking you are in a room where the same thing is going to happen over and over again. You have to have confidence in your ability to project what you bring with you into rehearsal out of your own life. You have to believe that this theatre space where we are improvising is not an artificial one lying outside life. What you normally have is a dreadful consensus that says: we are all going in there and we are going to transform ourselves. There has to be the possibility of its being different every day, because one's own state is different. That means improvising at the level of such a state, it doesn't imply leaving life behind you. One day, for example, you are incredibly happy, and then you will improvise out of this feeling of happiness. And another day, when you feel terrible, you will improvise out of this terrible state. This is how you might possibly strike it rich. If all one does is try desperately to reconstruct the improvisation one did the day before yesterday, which is already a fixed state, then that will no longer be an improvisation.

*Malgorzata Bartula*: That is how the *Play without a Title* [*Komödie ohne Titel*] begins. What is said there is that we are not in the theatre, we are in the midst of life.

*Roberto Ciulli*: Yes, that is Lorca's theme.

*Malgorzata Bartula*: That is the basic theme of your own work. If one is seeking continuous, creative, living theatre work, no exchange of realities must take place. Do you prefer particular situations when you improvise?

*Roberto Ciulli*: Improvisations are themselves improvised. You notice that during rehearsals, that's where it happens. We did Eduardo de Fillipo's play *I morti non fanno paura* [*Tote machen keine Angst*] for example. The play has a beginning, which is clear, it has an atmosphere, which is Italian, and a theme, which is death. A person has died. We have a gathering, a chap gives a meaningless speech – it's quite a simple story. We rehearsed that for three or four weeks and did not get anywhere. It was not bad, we could have put it on – it was theatre. And one evening I said as I always do: let's go through the text. The people sit around and simply speak their lines all the way through the text. And while they are memorising the text, while they are trying to think of nothing but the text and are quite empty of all other thoughts, I realise all of a sudden that this is the scene. This is exactly what a gathering after a funeral that has been going on for hours is like. They have all already eaten, they have had something to drink and now here they are. And someone has died. The quality of an actor who is only memorising the text is precisely that. So what emerges by accident is a real, extreme situation.

*Malgorzata Bartula*: Which is then very difficult to reconstruct consciously?

*Roberto Ciulli*: Yes. If I say, "now we are going to improvise a funeral," one won't necessarily get back to the core of that situation every time. And this is where I believe that the director is important because he has the opportunity to watch in a concentrated fashion and to react. Improvisation is a very radical idea for which no method can be evolved.

*Malgorzata Bartula*: From what you are saying it seems as though what theatre work is about is that tiny grain of sand between the stones, about displacing familiar perspectives. Which brings us back to the quality of life, if we were bold enough to accept it.

*Roberto Ciulli*: Improvisations are the moments when the human being has a sense of being at a distance from the situation as it normally is. That is the true alienation. Not in the Brechtian sense of the term. In life, too, it is like that: you find yourself in a very tragic situation and suddenly you fall out of your accustomed role. You stand over a freshly dug grave and you sing "Azzurro..." ["Blue..."], and everyone stares at you. At that moment a rift arises. Those are moments of liberation, the moments when the human being senses a distance to the action of which he is a part.

*Malgorzata Bartula*: I experienced that once in a plane. It was not even my first flight. All of a sudden I looked down on the perspective to which we are condemned. Why can't human beings fly? The flight of Icarus ended in death ... The word flight is used in the theatre: an actor flies, in the role...

*Roberto Ciulli*: ... or a play. Yes, and now we have landed back at the point where we realise there really is a parallel between the theatre and life.

*Malgorzata Bartula*: I say "fly", and you say "landed back at the point."

*Roberto Ciulli*: Yes, but don't fly too far.

FOURTH CONVERSATION

# Life Is the Most Difficult Art

*Malgorzata Bartula*: You regard the foundation of the *Junges Theater an der Ruhr* [The *Youth Theatre on the Ruhr*] in 1997 as the logical consequence of the basic idea of the *Theater an der Ruhr,* where finding oneself is the essential component.

*Roberto Ciulli*: This is precisely the point where one may situate the aesthetics and the whole political content of the *Theater an der Ruhr* – its whole history is the logical continuation of this beginning. Our theatre must now initiate projects which intervene in society.

*Malgorzata Bartula*: At the same time, opening up the theatre to young people is an old idea of yours.

*Roberto Ciulli*: The idea probably goes back to my own childhood. I think acting is one of the essential ways human beings adopt in seeking to initiate a process of self-recognition, to develop further. For through acting one can learn a lot about oneself and one can free oneself from outside influences. So the idea of establishing a *Junges Theater* within the *Theater an der Ruhr* as a free space for young people, where they can meet two or three times a week and act together regardless of whether they intend to become actors or not, is indeed an old one. The theatre exists as an institution with professional actors and so on, but it also has the task of motivating people to act. A society which acts together is certainly a society which is peaceful, which is humorous and which is tolerant.

*Malgorzata Bartula*: The term liberation is probably central to the idea of the *Junges Theater.* In the *Junges Theater* people come together who are at an age when this process of liberating oneself from all outside influences, from what they have hitherto experienced in the family, at school, in the way education is organised in our society, becomes decisive and difficult in their lives. All of us remember how we used to play together up to the age of seven and how that changed radically when we went to school. During the first school year playing was eliminated from the lives of children, so that by the second school year they were fit for routine work from which anything playful is alien. By the time young people have reached this point, another ten years have passed, and they are already very alienated from themselves. That is the result of educational policy and other social functionalisations. Accordingly, what emerges as the prime factor in our work at the *Junges Theater* is the refusal to fulfil functional expectations, to submit to pressure, to serve interests other than one's own.

*Roberto Ciulli*: That is one of the most difficult and decisive phases in a person's development. Emerging from a sheltered childhood, which offered a certain free space, even freedom to tell the truth, one runs up against a new, alien social order. This is a phase where one is exposed to the most diverse forms of manipulation and perhaps adopts a role one only many years later realises was superficial and was not something one took on through one's own free choice. It is for this reason that in this particular phase of one's life acting, acting in the theatre with the emphasis on improvisation, can have real importance, because improvising means putting oneself in a position where one has to make decisions all the time. This is, of course, basically what happens in life, too. A life without improvisation, a life where I take no decisions because these have already been taken for me, is a dead life. If, for example, I encounter a beggar I have to decide whether to give him anything or not. Most people simply walk past, because at that moment they do not want to make a decision. A human being only really lives if he takes conscious decisions all the time and then stands by them. In improvisation I exercise this ability to take decisions which every human being possesses as a gift and I can learn the significance of even the most minor decision. This also enables us to understand the value of life, to regard it as a treasure, where every minute, every small moment is of great significance. Young people are in a phase where they can still have experiences which will determine the rest of their lives. And acting in the theatre, improvising has this function for me. If I did not exercise moving my hands every morning I soon would not be able to do so. And if I do not practice taking decisions I soon will not know how to decide anything, certainly not politically. If all I ever do is stick my head in the sand, there will come a time when I will not even know what a decision looks like. For any society this is a quite dangerous development.

*Malgorzata Bartula*: You maintain that the *Junges Theater* is free of all types of pressure: from the pressure of time, from the stress of performance, from the obligation to deliver the goods. But the liberation you have described in the case of people who are no longer children, who are almost grown up, is a very difficult process which takes a lot of time. In your work you stress continuity, over long periods of time. But at the same time it is one of the principles of the *Junges Theater* that it reconstitutes itself with each new season and each new school year. Actually, one ought to refound it every year. I wonder whether you can have both options. A year is a long time, but it is not long enough to bring someone to the point where he will expose himself to an improvised situation freely, with self-awareness and courage, and will enjoy making decisions.

*Roberto Ciulli*: I think the question of time is relative. For what I have described as training people to make decisions we can only provide the stimulus. Someone who has practiced this kind of thing with us through improvisation over the course of a year will have had the great opportunity of understanding something for himself and of then further developing it elsewhere. To that extent a year in which he has become familiar with this kind of acting in this kind of situation can be of great importance for his life. It is generally recognised that it takes at least three years to train an actor or a theatre group. But I believe that for what we are trying to do with the *Junges Theater* even one year constitutes a relatively intensive period if one is thoroughly involved with it for many hours a week, as compared to the amount of time one spends with family or at school. This does not solve the problem you have spoken about, but is it in fact a problem? It is a Sisyphean task, but it always is. Enlightenment is a Sisyphean task, too, you always have to start from the beginning again. And I am even prepared to believe that this is the way it should be. In the theatre we start each new day, each rehearsal from the very beginning.

*Stefan Schroer*: From what you have been saying it seems that, on the one hand, a process begins each time anew, every encounter in acting is a fresh one. On the other hand, however, and in the light of that the idea of starting again from the very beginning does not sound particularly dynamic; you have described a process set in motion by improvisation, which is admittedly not linear, but which nevertheless contributes to a person's development. That is what we experienced in the *Junges Theater,* too. It did take quite a lot of time until someone had understood the possibilities which were open to him or her in that space, but then a process sets in, where the person begins to set a stamp on himself which, in ideal terms, is irreversible.

*Roberto Ciulli*: When I say from the very beginning I do not mean that everything has really been forgotten but that the person must be strict enough with himself always to dare to embark on a new beginning. The very beginning is a hypothesis I always have to assume. For example, I can say I have understood Kant's categorical imperative, I have comprehended it with my mind, and many years later I might even imagine I thought it up myself, although I know Kant did. And yet, if I concern myself with a moral question and have to act, I must constantly review whether I really do think like this and, thus, I have to think the question through even more profoundly. Beginning from the very beginning thus constitutes a working hypothesis, a hypothesis for life whereby the human being experiences everything he does as a new experience. That is Socrates' principle, and he took the position: I do not know a thing, please explain it to me. Although he already knew everything he asked about. This is quite the opposite of maintaining one already knows everything. There is always a way of knowing things one already knows which goes beyond the knowledge one believes one has finally attained. This curiosity constitutes the quality of life. As soon as I say I have developed to a particular point and have achieved this or that, I am maintaining there is something I no longer need. But the opposite is the case, one always needs everything.

*Stefan Schroer*: You used the example of acquiring a particular philosophical insight. But there is a difference between the process which is possible here and that which is grounded in a different relationship between knowledge and experience. It is certainly possible to assimilate philosophical ideas to the extent that it no longer matters whether they are the product of one's own mind or not, but it is incredibly difficult to represent through the senses a philosophy that one has perceived through and processed in the mind, i.e., really to influence one's character with philosophemes, in the positive sense that a subject is doing this and that in doing so he may become a mature subject.

*Roberto Ciulli*: Right, with the mind everything does go much more quickly, but the path from the mind to the heart, to experience, to life, that is the difficult process. Acting renders this process possible, it is precisely this path which improvisation opens up. For what one has understood only at the level of the understanding is of no use in life. Through acting I can reach the point where I myself determine how I behave towards myself and others and where I take the decisions. That is more than understanding, it is performing actions. And that is why I believe that acting in the theatre in this way is one of the most important methods of practising for life. One may argue about art, what art is and whether acting in the theatre is art or not, but life in this sense is the most difficult art.

*Malgorzata Bartula*: It is the declared intention of the *Theater an der Ruhr* to regard the actor as author, to have the actor speak his lines as though he had written them himself. With young people this is hardly possible, because what they are always performing is their own future, which is greater than their own fund of experience. So what emerges is something very attractive: a young actor chooses a text, he declares his desire to master it without actually being able to do so. He asserts his desire without achieving any unity with the text. Trying to do something with him, not seeking what has previously been achieved, but something short of that, the path to it – this revelation, the search is what I find valuable.

*Roberto Ciulli*: I am fundamentally against any strict categorisations which exclude material of quality. But there is a difference in the way professional actors perform and the way amateurs do. One is sometimes very surprised by the latter. It is their courage, their audacity, in asserting themselves. Whether it is young people, senior citizens or the sick who are performing theatre, all of them have a frank and courageous relationship with literature. There is a lot of poor taste and there will be some embarrassing moments – but there are also times which are quite astounding. These times are rare, the kind of thing you seldom find in established theatres. But no sooner has someone taken the decision to become an actor than he will begin to negate all of that in his mind.

*Roberto Ciulli*: There are not many models in society from which one can learn how collective intelligence or collective experience works. Since society is structured in the way it is, most of the models there are function in conditions of intolerance and authoritarianism, in prison actually. In prison the opportunity for collective experience exists, just as it does in schools. Wherever you look you will always come across models which are authoritarian in character. Society does not tolerate any free models of collectivity, since these bear an explosive force within them which endangers the political order of society. There are political parties, churches, sports clubs, but all of them reproduce in their structures the authoritarian structures of society. But what we have here is a model where one can experience without external pressure, as an individual and without that negative aspect of authority how a collective develops and how it functions.

*Malgorzata Bartula*: I have to question your use of the word "without". For what we are doing here is essentially an interaction between people asserting themselves, which is authoritarian and dictatorial, and people refusing to do so.

*Roberto Ciulli*: You are talking about mechanisms within the collective itself, not about pressure from outside. There is a difference. I am talking about an atmosphere free of such external pressure, which is free of the pressure to achieve you find in sports clubs which leads to the exclusion of an individual if he doesn't fit in or of collectives which can only function in terms of a huge external discipline such as group therapy which the members are indirectly forced to participate in. The *Junges Theater*, by contrast, is a voluntary affair, and you are not some kind of external authority pushing the collective into doing something particular; what you do is allow something to emerge. Of course, in such a free organisation phenomena occur which move in this direction too, but this happens from within the group.

*Malgorzata Bartula*: Yes. Yet even in a space free of constraints the experiences people bring into it are reflected. Which is why there is also the question of the time, since there may indeed be an external freedom, but nevertheless what is reflected here is what we all bring with us. On the one hand, I always have to take account of what people bring with them, on the other I am equally concerned to refuse to instrumentalize it.

*Roberto Ciulli*: It is dangerous when everyone has theatre in his mind, because one is actually in a theatre. One sees the performance, one experiences theatre. It is naturally very difficult to develop within the theatre a world of one's own which does not abide by the categories of acting theatre. Because you too have theatre in your head, I do too, as I observe you, it is incredibly difficult. But what the young people, who are not actors, do in the *Junges Theater* must be absolutely free from any kind of evaluation in terms of theatrical categories. Only then will we see its strength, because here we are not concerned with the aesthetics of the theatre, but with something quite different. This is very difficult, and it is not something one can achieve right away. Every year the *Junges Theater* is a new project, but it will grow with experience and will reach this point sometime. That is an ongoing process for all of us.

*Roberto Ciulli*: There are two phases of work in each project of the *Junges Theater*, and these have to be distinguished from one another. There is a phase where we act in this space, a phase where we live in terms of the hypothesis of the space, regardless of whether we are working on a theatre play or not. Then there is the phase where one goes before the public. But if you go before the public only because one is in a theatre, one is taking a step backwards because one is regarding what one is making public only as a theatrical performance. One has to ask oneself: "why are we making this public and what is it for?" That is a question addressed to the young people to: "Why am I going before the public? For whom? What for? What is the message? What am I showing? Am I showing something of myself? Am I showing what I have been doing for six months in a small space?" If one attempts to answer such questions, one will see that it is simply not enough to answer at the level of saying: "I am putting on a play, I am mounting a production." The question 'why' is more profound than that. Going public introduces a new quality, a new aim, and that must be done consciously and described. Over the time I have been watching them the young people have been getting more interesting, each one of them individually, each one in a different way, and together they form a fine constellation. But in the end there has to be this debate with each individual, quite strictly: "What do you intend when you show this to other people? Why are you doing this? For whom?"

*Stefan Schroer*: One possible answer to these questions could be that a performance extends the process you have been describing by the motive involved in talking about one's self and about one's own life. Not in any real sense, but as a making known of a way of seeing things, of a specific perspective, which in our society has neither significance nor power.

*Roberto Ciulli*: Agreed. But that can only come about if one works without the premise that at some point I am going to go public with what is being created in this work. It means working in order to acquire an experience, even about a play, without thinking that at some point this is going to be put on. And then comes the moment when out of the many themes of the play one theme crystallises which is of central concern to the group, where something arises which expresses a specific interest of theirs, freed from the givens of the literary text, along with a view of the world. And then a moment may come where one says to oneself: now we have something, this is what we must put on.

*Malgorzata Bartula*: The performances which have taken place up to now have led me to feel and realise what the transformation of people in the *Junges Theater* is all about. Their original, naïve desire, their general knowledge and the equally universal curiosity they have brought with them has become – in individually different ways – more specific. Over this period their decisions in the improvisations have become less arbitrary and the imprints of the persons clearer. And the very fact of the performances is going to be processed by them, the process will continue.

FIFTH CONVERSATION

# Life Belongs to the Actor

*Malgorzata Bartula*: Who decides which situation lends itself to improvisation, the director or the actor?

*Roberto Ciulli*: I don't think that matters. What does matter is the theme, which must be precisely defined before starting out. Who decides what it is doesn't matter. If you are working with a group of human beings who are familiar with this way of acting, the impetus for an improvisation may be quite accidental, it is certainly very open. The stronger the people doing the improvisation, the more clearly they will define their creativity, the more the theme of the improvisation will be clarified during the acting process. The weaker they are, the less experience they have had, the more precisely you will have to define the theme. In the best case it is like life itself: a situation comes about by chance and its structure emerges while it is actually going on.

*Malgorzata Bartula*: You once said that you didn't want to kill off life in the theatre any longer, you didn't want to have any corpses in the cellar. Through improvisation you are embarking with your actors on a journey into the unknown. The improvisation proceeds, a situation develops. But who then decides whether what takes place there is a living situation, and who decides when it is over? How many breaks do you allow during acting?

*Roberto Ciulli*: What you can experience in the hypothetical space of the theatre over five hours does not at all correspond to five hours of waiting in real life. In life you would need ten years to realise this potential experience, and the breaks would last for years. That is a question of deciding to exist in another time. The question of patience also arises in this relationship. Nevertheless, no one usually brings it up, because everyone is thinking about the result, the première, external time. In relation to six weeks rehearsal time five hours appears a lot. Actors and directors must together free themselves from these external constraints by gaining confidence in a method of acting which is not dictated by the result. But then who decides when the improvisation is over? Even in such a constellation of people those who do this are mostly those watching, for they are responsible for what acting elicits from the audience. The actors are responsible for what happens between those acting. They may be richly rewarded during acting, it is those on the outside who are the yardstick as to whether this is also communicated to them.

*Malgorzata Bartula*: Actors always find it difficult to interrupt an improvisation, they only do so in extreme cases, don't they?

*Roberto Ciulli*: Yes, because an interruption always implies failure. That is why the actors always try to overcome such a moment. They prefer the interruption to come from outside.

*Malgorzata Bartula*: You mentioned trust and you said that the basic prerequisite for the work is that the actors trust you. Do you trust the actors?

*Roberto Ciulli*: I work in such a way as to create such trust. If one has worked together for a while one can tell whether an actor is cheating or not during improvisation. If I become aware of that I try to correct or clarify it during the work. With actors who don't cheat I don't need to do that. I also trust them in the sense that everyone who begins an improvisation has to be given a chance. Even if someone is not entirely open, not quite honest, he has a right to become so. I have trust in relation to time and to the possibility which each actor has to open up to the collective and to the work.

*Malgorzata Bartula*: To use the time.

*Roberto Ciulli*: In my work I am noticing more and more that my trust takes me a long way and the actors are more ready to close the door than I am. I leave it open for a long time. But then situations occur where this becomes impossible because others do not have the patience to do so.

*Malgorzata Bartula*: If you improvise on a text – and you say that this form of improvisation opens up the richest possibilities – does the actor find his own way into the text or is it the other way round? At some point the first word has to be spoken.

*Roberto Ciulli*: I don't think you can make that distinction. It is as you describe it, the first word has to be spoken. It happens that an actor improvises but the text does not come. It simply refuses to come. And then the actor does manage to create a situation where he really can speak the first line, which he has not written. The actor is stronger than the text, he appropriates it. The text has no subjectivity, it just stands there lifeless, it is dead. Life belongs to the actor. It is a question of the actor empathising with the text. That is why in this unending series of possibilities it is rather the actor who finds his way to the text. Faust examines Mephisto's body and at some point he finds this text, which was there before his eyes, abstract, outside him. Suddenly he finds a way through to it, through the senses, through a vein, through something in the body.[1] The process is an acting one.

*Malgorzata Bartula*: One prerequisite for the success of the acting is how the characters are cast. When you consider that in advance, are you guided by a person's anxiety, which he has to overcome or by the utopia he hopes to realise?

*Roberto Ciulli*: If we are beginning we must already have conceived the material in such a way that we know what direction it is moving in. Casting is determined by the notion of what one wants to achieve with the characters. The work always remains open, but this is clear before. Casting, and for that matter the decision with regard to the gender of a character, is part of the basic conception of the work.

*Malgorzata Bartula*: If you want to realise not only the conception of a production but also the human dimension of the work it is not

---

[1] In the production of *Margarete Faust*, the Second Part of the *Faust* Trilogy as performed by the *Theater an der Ruhr* (the première was in November 1998) the Walpurgis Night (*Walpurgisnacht*) scene takes place in a morgue. At the beginning of this scene, Faust dissects the body of Mephisto laid out on an operating table.

only the development of the characters which matters but also the human beings themselves. For the actors to share your vision, they have to be aware of a personal challenge. If they had to overcome anxieties before starting that would be negative, it would be more positive if they envisaged some utopian aim.

*Roberto Ciulli*: Theatre will only work on the basis of freedom from anxieties. Only then will actors be able to act. Of course every human being has many anxieties, most of them are fairly superficial. But when you go on stage you have to be entirely free of them. That is why the whole acting process constitutes a freedom from anxieties. The anxieties we are talking about are anxieties which have been there previously, but which one has freed oneself from. The decision to become an actor is a decision to free oneself from anxieties. And this is where theatre participates in society. The theatre is a social and political space which gives society the opportunity to free itself and it initiates a process aimed at destroying authority – through liberating one's own forces, through developing them in a way that cannot be stopped. In Heiner Müller's *Landschaft mit Argonauten* Jason says: A pack of actors marches by in step CAN'T YOU SEE THEY ARE DANGEROUS THEY ARE ACTORS.

*Malgorzata Bartula*: You have now been working in Germany for many years with people who apparently do not have any economic worries. How do you make clear to them that need exists, that the heavens can in fact fall in on them? Individualism, which has emerged historically as a positive utopia in terms of the sovereignty of the individual and the destruction of authority, can be seen as degenerate. What I see is a mass consisting of apparent individualists, which is wholly occupied with its private concerns. This is a false, apolitical individualism. It does not serve to concentrate power. What seems most difficult today is bringing forces together to realise an idea, an idea of something higher than themselves, something which means more, like love. How do you communicate to such people the necessity to come together in support of an idea, to live for it?

*Roberto Ciulli*: That is very difficult. Particularly since we are at a juncture where we have to give shape to the new century using formulations we still have to find. Of course, there are constants in historical development, but on the whole it is a dynamic process. In the eighteenth and nineteenth centuries they struggled to liberate the slaves. That aim was achieved. But then you discover that slavery, the division of human beings into a first and a second category, still persists. It is a constant, as is the struggle against it. Only the struggle for the twenty-first century cannot be fought using categories of struggle from previous centuries. The struggle is a constant, but the means and the opportunities change. Today, rapid change is taking place throughout society. That makes it difficult to find exactly the right strategy. Pressure from materialism is seen to be increasing when compared with other values such as solidarity. Particularly in Germany, where wealth has emerged from the catastrophe of the Second World War, social conditions are very immobile.

How do you define need? Marxism is a great idea, a vision, but we have left it behind us. And thus also its content, the insight which is common to both Christianity and Marxism, namely that human beings are working together for something that will come in the future. Today the idea that life does not only mean working for yourself and taking responsibility for your personal future is discredited. Deciding that there will be no such thing as the future is simple enough. It is more difficult to proceed from the notion that there will be a future. You say it is difficult to work in a country like Germany. But it is more important than working in a country where people are willing to exercise solidarity with one another from the start. Making theatre depends on where you are. I am against exporting theatre and culture and against directors flying to Cameroon, directing *Antigone* there and then flying out again. I go abroad and I see that local conditions there are different. That is why I have always rejected such offers. For me producing theatre in another country means deciding to live there. You have to differentiate within Germany, too. Hamburg is different from Berlin, and from Mülheim. The aim is to change the place where you are. Career-mindedness is awful. The ghosts which have not yet arrived at any one place are the most dreadful.

*Malgorzata Bartula*: You describe theatre as a political event. This development of the individual may be seen on the one hand as a positive thing, as a liberation from usurpers, slavery, alienation; on the other hand, people fall victim to the decisions of the banks, the stock exchange and big business, which is to say that alienation is a constant. The private, the nihilistic, and the apolitical is what is concealed from us. Improvisation changes the quality of life subjectively. And objectively? What is the political nature of theatre? Where is it directly effective, other than in the subjective realm? You say, in improvisation actions are interchangeable. But reality implies actions which cannot be interchanged, like war. And it swamps theatre. That is what the theatre has to anticipate.

*Roberto Ciulli*: Theatre can change reality. Can. It can even form the centre of a revolutionary movement.

*Malgorzata Bartula*: Which has happened in history.

*Roberto Ciulli*: Which has actually happened. But that is not the main thing. Theatre seldom achieves any great political effect, because unlike political agitation, it is not directed at the mass of the population. Actually it serves to undermine the mass through the effect it has on the individual person. But this is precisely where its opportunity lies. In contrast to the political mass, which can always be manipulated, theatre constitutes social change through changing individual human beings. It intervenes in the most intimate sphere of the human being, and from here it can have great effect. Like a virus, a creeping sickness which affects all the family.

SIXTH CONVERSATION

# Working on the Creation of Something New in the Green Fields

*Stefan Schroer:* In the course of one of the "Nights in the Theatre" under the title *Zum ewigen Frieden* [*Toward Eternal Peace*][1] you described the policy responsible for NATO's war on Yugoslavia as "an ever-repeating scenario with a fixed distribution of roles." Nevertheless, these repetitions do imply a development which might be described as an ongoing process of establishing the so-called "new world order." In your contributions to those "Nights in the Theatre" you characterised such a development as fatal not only in terms of its external, military consequences but also of the internal structure of our ostensibly democratically organised society where legitimate politics are losing all semblance of autonomy. The *Theater an der Ruhr* countered the kind of political development which became apparent during that war in a more intense form by setting up a forum for political debate. This was a more direct counterpart to your artistic work, the creative work you have been describing by which the actor and by analogy the audience, too, becomes a more autonomous subject, which is more capable of political action. How, then, are we to describe in concrete terms the political influence of a theatre conceived and practiced in this way in the face of a social development which seeks not only to replace the autonomous political space but also to oust its advocates, the responsible subjects, from the arena of political efficacy?

---

[1] During the NATO bombing raids on Yugoslavia, which took place from March to May 1999, the *Theater an der Ruhr* regularly hosted public discussions on the war and its consequences under the title - borrowed from Kant - of *Toward Eternal Peace*.

*Roberto Ciulli*: I speak in the name of the theatre, and within the theatre we advocate a particular direction, which is, however, related to other, similarly constituted efforts at all levels of society. In its general development, and particularly in the education system, society is not achieving the target we are aiming at, but there are many people working in the same direction as we are. Not only in the theatre, not only in the arts, but in all sectors of society, in politics too, even within the establishment. We no longer have opposing blocks based on different functions, we have a transversal line right across the social spectrum. In the theatre, for example, two blocks would form in political matters as well: on the one side were the artists and on the other, the technicians. Today these blocks no longer exist. What you find today regarding peoples' political positions is a transversal unity, independent of such blocks. Particular artists come together with particular technicians, and vice versa. The fact that what we have today is links between the different sections of society, the fact that alliances are possible between people who exercise different functions in society, is a new quality which can only further the kind of development we are advocating. A second reason why our artistic work will become more directly political in future lies in the effects of recent technological developments such as information science and communications, globalisation, and the ability to travel. In their first phase these tend to serve negative tendencies within society. Greater access to information facilitates propaganda, globalisation provides a means for capital and for the big concerns to extend their power on a global scale, the ability to travel initially favours a kind of imperialist tourism. All technological development goes through a first phase like this. But there is a second phase which follows on the zenith of the first. Developments in the media, for instance, have reached the height of their negative influence. For many people they were exposed as propaganda first in the Gulf War and then in Kosovo. People realised that there were particular interests behind them. And so you get an awareness which can undermine the negative tendency and bring out the positive potential of such technology. Twenty years ago, when these new developments in the media surprised us all, such an awareness did not exist. These two factors: the transversal possibilities in society and the changes in technological development, this second positive phase which is following on the negative results of the first, and is now beginning – these two elements indicate that there is a possibility of changing society in the direction we have been working towards. But the theatre cannot do this alone.

*Stefan Schroer*: In both cases you have described to us the impulse for change proceeds from people who think and act. In what you called the "ever repeating scenario with a fixed distribution of roles" it is not the roles of Clinton or Blair we have in mind, but the more functional roles. Does that not mean that the real problem lies in desubjectivization and thus in the depoliticization of the social space, so that the person who acts autonomously, if he exists and can be strengthened through the kind of processes you have been describing, is confronted by an abstract machinery of power and by the interests of capital which are now operating almost independently?

*Roberto Ciulli*: The repetition of this scenario, too, is taking place in different phases. We have encountered phenomena such as the de-individualisation of human beings, such as power, the interests of capital and the globalisation tendencies a number of times in history already. It has often been the case that power structures emerge and societies are formed which deprive people of freedom. You have to distinguish between lack of freedom in the $19^{th}$ century and lack of freedom in the $20^{th}$, between the lack of freedom in countries which have no economic power and lack of freedom in economically strong countries. This scenario and its apparently unalterable development always exist in one direction only, however. But then all of a sudden something new comes up. It begins with a message, in a group, through a book or an article. Or with a madman who maintains he is the Messiah, and at first only twelve people believe him. Or someone proposes that the work human beings perform is alienated and he writes a couple of pages about it. It is such impulses which suddenly give rise to something new. And this impetus is always provided by a particular person. It is an open question as to which country and which period this happens in, we don't know. The important thing, however, is that people do their work without exactly knowing whether the womb is fruitful. If they are not part of written history, then they belong to unwritten history.

*Stefan Schroer*: Within such a scenario where lies the work of the theatre such as you understand it and have described it to us in these conversations? Is it preparing the womb or would it rather be what falls into one's lap?

*Roberto Ciulli*: Both. We are the ones doing the sensitising, we are performing the preparatory work. But whether a member of the audience feels he is being addressed, whether someone is being sensitised and decides to pass this experience on to others, we do not know. We are, however, working in a field where something like this is possible. In the drought-stricken landscape of theatre there are some fields where water is present and which therefore enable us to plant something, to give birth to something. And in society, as in theatre, there are a number of dry landscapes, and there are some green patches, too, where something new might arise. It can happen there, it can happen with us. It used to be important in what region of the globe something like this happened, as with Gandhi in India. But today Gandhi has become a universal phenomenon. To South Africa Nelson Mandela was what Gandhi was to India, but today such a phenomenon is universal at the same time. Where it actually began does not matter. But it can only happen at a particular moment. Only at the appropriate time, at a concrete location, in association with people who are moved by the same thing, is it able to break up the power structure of a society which has ossified. Who knows whether we can create such a moment through our work or whether we will encounter such a time? In our lives, however, it is a precious thing to know that we are working on the right side, that with our strength and our life's work we are not merely going on supporting a theatre which is already dead, that we are not mindlessly performing pointless work in drought-stricken fields, but that we are working on the creation of something new in the green fields.

SEVENTH CONVERSATION

# Theatre for the Outsider

*Malgorzata Bartula*: One aspect of the history of the *Theater an der Ruhr* project has been the development of a new theatre language.

*Roberto Ciulli*: Not so much a new language as a consensus regarding certain terms we have defined more precisely. If someone speaks of realism, we know what is meant. Or improvisation, if you like.

*Malgorzata Bartula*: When certain terms become the focus of attention, then from that point on language organises itself anew.

*Roberto Ciulli*: In terms of the language of the theatre with which we are all familiar our language is new to the extent that we are pursuing an interdisciplinary working project where language does not relate solely to theatre work. We began this at the end of the 1970s with the structural model of the *Theater an der Ruhr*. Then came the idea of internationalisation, which went much further than we had originally envisaged. What was important, too, was our third idea, namely that in our theatre work, in putting together new productions, we would also need research. Research thus becomes part of the theatre, whose main object is communication, the power to express oneself. Philosophy, psychology, sociology and history all flowed into our work, they have left their imprint on the language adopted between the director and the actors in rehearsals. We tried to use all these elements to explode the provincialism of theatre. So we tried to open up our work to other disciplines. If we happen on Freud when we are working on a play like Ibsen's *House*,[1] we suspend the rehearsals for a while and have a look at

---

[1] Ibsen's *House* is a collage of scenes from Ibsen's plays.

Freud. If in dealing with *The Lower Depths* or *The Exception and the Rule* [*Die Ausnahme und die Regel*] we encounter the master-servant problem, then we set about discussing Hegel's *Phenomenology of Spirit* and *The Dialectic of the Enlightenment*.

*Stefan Schroer*: The interesting thing about the communication processes going on in rehearsal is the transformations which take place. Unlike most philosophical discussions which function interpretatively and bring things to a point where they can assume an independent existence, dialogue in rehearsal functions in such a way that theoretical knowledge becomes the impulse for something new.

*Roberto Ciulli*: That's the good thing about the link between philosophy and the theatre. The first commandment in theatre is sensuality. We have to create something sensual. The actors are driven by a desire to give abstractions sensual form, to crystallise a precise thought from philosophical theory and through that a feeling, the sensuality of ideas. The work of the actor lies in thinking. Acting is thinking. Here lies the link.

*Stefan Schroer*: But it is not just a question of the sensualization of a philosophical or theoretical notion, but more of an impulse, which opens up a further improvisatory quest.

*Roberto Ciulli*: True. It goes further. We are living, even if we are doing so in the hypothetical space of the theatre. Intellectual impulses become practical reality by becoming part of life, by being born. All of a sudden, and that is the good thing about it, theory becomes very concrete, it becomes real. It gets contradicted, too. Perhaps that is the essential thing about our work.

*Malgorzata Bartula*: Since the mid-nineties the ensemble has been in process of reconstruction, as has the repertoire. New actors join us, new plays are presented, old ones are revived, different casts take over. How does language work for new actors, how successful is the communication?

*Roberto Ciulli*: When a role is recast, this is not done along the lines of the recasting model other theatres adopt. In our case this does not simply imply taking over what had been done hitherto, simply by switching the people involved, but it implies incorporating the life of the person now playing the role into the conceptual structure of the production. Even when we are recasting we leave space for the creativity of the actor. This is the first time we have decided to revive a production. I am referring to a production whose content we think works independently of time and place. There are a number of productions like this which we did in the 1980s, which were done too soon, where we were not only up with the times, but well ahead of them. So we had a lot of difficulty with the plays, they were not fully understood. I have always refused to do revivals, because it looks as though one is cultivating one's repertoire or looking for ways of preserving plays one happens to like. When we founded the *Theater an der Ruhr* the idea was to find a group of fifteen to twenty people which would remain together and evolve a design for living. It would not just be a project for five years' work in the theatre. We already had a group then. If you begin like that you develop a discourse which goes on for years. I could not imagine then that after a few years the usual changes in the ensemble and the repertoire would take place in our theatre, too. We kept to the basic idea for more than ten years. Then something happened we had not foreseen. Psychology took over, marginal matters suddenly became central, and the work became routine. At that point we knew we would have to change something, that it would be false to go on living as though nothing had happened. So we made a radical break and decided to found the theatre all over again, since the constellation of people we then had was not working. Today we have a new constellation of people – it certainly did not come about by chance, a lot of work was involved – with whom we are rethinking the whole project of the *Theater an der Ruhr*, just as we did at the beginning. That is why today we have come round to putting on revivals of plays which – had we not made the break at that time – would still have been in the repertoire: *Kaspar* and *Tote ohne Begräbnis* [*Morts sans Sépulture*] – performances which offer a platform for communication anywhere in the world.

*Malgorzata Bartula*: *Kaspar* thematises the potential for violence in language.

*Roberto Ciulli*: Handke's text was written as an attack on fascism in the German media in 1968. We extended Handke's critique of language by the dimension of its violent use in education and in the media. Mistrust of language which leads to alienation and prevents any awareness of self, language deployed as a system – that is what the story of Kaspar is about, someone (in our case the someone was a woman, since Maria Neumann played Kaspar) who was violently injected with language. Politics provides a good example of this. Today we know that education is falsely conceived. The erosion of political language has apparently continued, too. There is a public debate going on about that today. The question has been posed, so we must think it through anew. In this point *Kaspar* is modern, it has not lost anything of its quality.

*Stefan Schroer*: This takes us back to the process of communication in rehearsal. If the director is the prompter, then the actor is a Kaspar who is subject to a despotic director and in the end cannot do anything of his own. How do you talk to actors when you are trying to communicate an idea, I don't mean in a manner which is alien to the body of the actor, but rather as an idea which is recreated in him, in his own language?

*Roberto Ciulli*: I have made it plain here that I used to be a perfect prompter. For years. Until I asked myself what I was actually doing and decided to change the relationship between the director and the actors.

*Stefan Schroer*: How can one still speak if that is the case?

*Roberto Ciulli*: I communicate with actors about ideas, about content, but never about the way these are to be expressed. I try to formulate my thoughts as clearly as possible. If you work together over a long period, one part of the content will already have been defined and you will only have to remind them of it. As to how to transpose an idea to the stage I allow for a lot of freedom. At the same time I naturally develop my own notions, images arise in my head. I see them. They are my images. I pass these on cautiously, in an associative way, as if by accident, as though they weren't particularly important, so that the actor does not begin to think: this is how he wants it, so this is the way I shall have to do it. And now there are a number of different possibilities. Either the actor is a complete subject, his head is empty, he doesn't have any ideas of his own, and he thus seizes on your image and does only what you have told him. Or he is an actor with a strong sense of self and he is annoyed that you are passing on an image to him. The first thing he does is to think up a counter-image. He does precisely what you have not suggested. You say, he can go and have a smoke. He says, fine, then he comes and has a drink. He just switches actions. But an actor who is free seizes on the idea I have in my head and adds something to this idea which was not there before. Because I am one person and he is another. If it catches on then something is created which has something to do with my idea but which is not only this. And if I am frank and watch, if I do not only concentrate on my own idea, if I have confidence in what I see, then what I get back is quite a different possibility. And so it goes on. It is both partners who improvise in a way. That means, I improvise too, and not only the actor. This is how I understand directing, as a counterpart to the kind of prompting which has become accepted in the theatre and which is still not being called into question in any fundamental way. This is the reason why no creative collective work is taking place and as a consequence of that why nothing is being created in the minds of the audience. What is being produced is dead theatre.

*Malgorzata Bartula*: You see yourself as a pioneer of an actor's theatre which is urgently necessary. Is this the end of director's theatre?

*Roberto Ciulli*: What I am interested in is a fundamentally new understanding of theatre, but I am not a theorist. During the years I have been working in theatre I have developed a theory of acting, but at a living level. I am myself the mediator, as a person. I formulate what I want in the course of the rehearsal. I do not simply produce plays, but with each new play some basic research work takes place. And that has not got through to the outside. Up to now there has not been any systematisation of this theory, nor has there been any transformation of its contents into another system which could make it the material for other theatre work. The reception of our work in theatre takes place within the framework of the standard view of theatre. It proceeds from the notion that we are an ordinary theatre, better than others perhaps, but not essentially different. The only way I can reach the wider public is by formulating what I think in interviews. But this theme can't really be put over in a newspaper interview. And then there is the problem that language as spoken, and certainly as acted, is something different from language as written.

*Malgorzata Bartula*: On the one hand you have not composed any manifesto to call for something new, but on the other there is an aspect of the *Theater an der Ruhr* where this idea does reach the outside and where a formulation in terms of the stage – but also off stage – does take place. That is the idea of travelling. The *Theater an der Ruhr* not only takes its productions to the German provinces, it also travels to other countries, indeed to other continents, beyond its linguistic borders. That, in particular, is where the *Theater an der Ruhr* has enjoyed unique success, as when you took *Kaspar* to South America in 1992 or *Morts sans Sépulture* to Turkey in 1990 and to Chile in 1992. The principle of dialogue in rehearsal – formulating ideas but not the way they should be expressed – is a principle you also follow in your international work. Even when you go to Uzbekistan and tell theatre practitioners there that they certainly should not imitate us but develop their own ideas.

*Roberto Ciulli*: Linking our idea of theatre to our international work has produced some wonderful moments which are much more important than any publicity about our work, which has not yet taken place in the appropriate manner. Most of these moments happen somewhere else, only a few of them at home. But those we reach through the language of this theatre are always the outsiders. People who feel they are outsiders, independently of their race, their nationality or their religion. For the Germans here at home there are lots of theatres, the *Theater an der Ruhr* has always been a theatre for the Germans who are outsiders, for those who feel like outsiders in Germany. It is the theatre which twenty years ago addressed the generation of young people in Mülheim living in the kind of family where the grandfather had been in the SS or the German army. In the seventies a young man would suffer from the fact that this theme was taboo at home. So then he would come to the theatre and he would feel we were addressing him. We addressed such people in other countries, too. The people in Chile we reached with *Morts sans Sépulture* felt they were outsiders in their own country because there was a cloak of silence over torture and the participation of doctors in torture. Those people felt that actually all of them were the tortured or the torturers, but the generally accepted belief was that the question should be left alone. And then along comes the *Theater an der Ruhr* and suddenly the people who were so very alienated in their country notice that here is a theatre talking their language. That is the basic idea behind our international work. We are not a theatre which is practising globalisation in the way it is usually understood today. This theatre speaks to those who feel they are outsiders in Germany in the same way it does to those who feel like outsiders in Chile or in Uzbekistan or in Iran. And there are some great moments during these encounters where you become aware that outsiders have come together and are communicating through the performance. In such a situation you do not have to explain anything. For us and the audience the performance of *Kaspar* we gave at the *Uemocucho* in Ecuador was a shared experience which has become part of our lives. Just as was our experience with *Kaspar* in a former hospital in Quito, a place with a terrible past, a place of death. The performances of *Morts sans Sépulture* in Turkey were similar. And finally the performances in Teheran in 1999 and 2000. The audiences there were comprised of people who live in a fundamentalist state but who feel they are part of a movement against that doctrine. Something took place there which could no longer be stopped. People understood something there which went far beyond any theoretical text about the nature of acting.

*Stefan Schroer*: *The Silk Road Project* [*Seidenstraßen-Projekt*]² contains the idea that one should feed precisely on such moments. The experience of such a successful encounter which changes both sides is intended in this project to flow directly into an open performance. Might one therefore regard *The Silk Road Project* as the manifesto you never wrote?

*Roberto Ciulli*: Basically the *Theater an der Ruhr* has made international work part of its program. This is designed as an encounter with the outsider and as an encouragement to living with those who feel they are outsiders, internationally and in their own country. What is the significance of *The Silk Road Project* beyond that? Many years ago this was no doubt a fantastic idea, but now it has become a necessity for me. For I believe that as far as possible we theatre practitioners should attempt to turn every person who comes into the theatre into a cosmopolitan. Everyone who leaves the theatre must be able to say: I am cosmopolitan. We must develop this potential to the furthest extreme possible. This is the consciousness with which we travel to other countries where, partly as a result of European policies exported there, a development in quite the opposite direction is taking place; new national states are arising and people are proud to be Uzbeks and not Russians. Here our only aim can be to work against such tendencies. In Uzbekistan eighty percent of the people you meet are nationalists, the other twenty percent suddenly feel alienated, they hardly recognise their own country any more. This new minority comprises intellectuals, authors, artists, actors. They are isolated and have run out of strength. In this situation the task of a theatre which speaks their language is to produce bastards. In general, international work is understood in such a way that one exports German national theatre

---

[2] The *Silk Road Project* consists essentially in working on a production with which the ensemble of the *Theater an der Ruhr* can then tour along the historical Silk Road from Europe to Asia. The idea came up as early as 1990, while the Theatre was giving performances in Turkey. Since then the *Theater an der Ruhr* has worked continuously on the realisation of this project by intensifying its links along the Silk Road and establishing new ones, as well as by touring to the region and inviting theatres from there to come to Mülheim. The kind of multilingual and intercultural production we are seeking will be created on this journey, as a result of an encounter with other cultures and their direct influence on the production.

to such regions, so that the people there will admire the German language and German culture. The Uzbeks, for their part, think the same, they send their national art to us. This is based on a completely false conception of what is one's own and what is foreign. We have to resolve this. We have to take away peoples' fear of losing their culture. I am not going to weep because no one here speaks Latin any more. No one suffers, so what is all the fuss about? Cultures come and go, they merge. There is something positive about dissolving national and cultural identities. This is a dynamic process which should not provoke anxieties.

*Stefan Schroer*: In terms of the intercultural work carried on by the *Theater an der Ruhr* one could view the theme of *Kaspar* somewhat differently. In purely theoretical language it is very difficult to construct a genuine dialogue or polylogue, to make associations with an encounter which is not instrumental without what one is saying becoming quite indifferent. In this case it is the theatre which can initiate the different forms of dialogue between cultures and between people of different cultures which are necessary today.

*Roberto Ciulli*: Yes. The language of theatre is different. Painting and music have no spoken language at all. But when I read a novel or a short story, its language cannot be separated from what I associate with it, from my associations. And language in the theatre is not purely rational or functional. The opportunity for the language of the theatre is that what is available to it is not just the rational meaning of objective understanding. In the theatre language retains its mysteries. The relativizing, the questioning of purely verbal understanding is quite a significant experience which helps us to open up new languages. It often happens that two people will understand each other a lot better through a silence than through lots of words. Language can also constitute an obstacle to understanding, which is something theatre recognises. In our case this occurs through multilingualism, through working with actors whose mother tongue is not the one they use on stage. How erotic the German language becomes when it is spoken by a foreigner!

The theatre can make this level of language accessible again, by means of actors working with it sensually. Language also has to do with recognition, however. That is why our audiences are often irritated when they hear an important line of Goethe's spoken by a foreigner on stage in a quite impossible accent. That greatly offends someone who knows this language very well. But this type of offence makes me aware of something else. I mean the achievement of immigrants. For it is the immigrants who transform the language of those who live here into a new treasure, a new vision. If you think that language is a yardstick of communication it forces you to speak in terms of being understood. That brings about a process of alienation. I notice this frequently with the foreigners who work with me. They become greatly alienated when they are under pressure to use the language correctly in a dialogue according to its own rules. Instead of submitting to the dominance of the prompter, each person should be accepted for his own language. We all speak German, but the person who dares to speak his own German is punished for it. So he has to give up part of himself. What we should be advocating in the theatre, on the other hand, is the right to individuality, the right to one's own personality, the right to speak a language of one's own. A person is not complete unless he has discovered his own language. It doesn't matter whether we are talking about a German or someone of a different nationality. What matters here is the concept of the outsider set free from his geographical moorings. In every society the outsider is the one who asserts a language of his own. The theatre is the place for this outsider.

*Malgorzata Bartula*: A person becomes an outsider at the point where someone says, I have not understood you. We are dealing with a language which is functional, whose concern is the readability of life, the transparency of the world. One word matches another one to one. In the theatre, however, there is a whole human being behind a spoken word. And what is projected into the word will remain a secret. The word is used but it is not at all transparent. Why is it so difficult in theatre to formulate an appeal for a willingness to communicate from secret to secret?

*Roberto Ciulli*: Because theatre is a dirty art.

*Malgorzata Bartula*: Because of sullied language? Because of human inconsistencies full of contradictions and suffering?

*Roberto Ciulli*: Because from the very beginning the creative process is wrapped up in political and economic contexts, whereas the creative process of the painter or the composer functions – at the beginning at least – completely independently of these categories. Actors, directors, stage designers begin their work in a space which is defined by strict structures. We have always been working in a context which limits our artistic freedom. That is why theatre has developed as it has. If you go back to Molière, you will see that even he could not write as he wanted to. The history of theatre is a history of the censorship of the mind or of the conscious attempt to instrumentalise theatre artists. One of the few who nevertheless tried to lay claim to his freedom was Artaud. The freedom of the theatre always exists in theory. All the great theatrical projects have failed so badly that we do not even know what they were. For that reason it is necessary to develop structures which enable us to exercise such freedom in practice too. The history of the theatre is characterised by this dirt, by the compromises inscribed in it from the start. It is in this framework that theatre developed historically. This is why it was so important for me to link the idea of a different kind of theatre work with the actual founding of a theatre. A fundamentally new development can only take place within new structures which permit free, collective creative development. Only in such structures can the kind of theatre we are talking about emerge and thrive.

EIGHTH CONVERSATION

# Myself as a Member of the Audience

*Roberto Ciulli*: The second part of our production of *Kaspar* contains a negative vision of the future. It portrays a family with three children and two servants as well as a beggar who have regressed to a primitive, animal-like state, and are dumb. This is a society which has lost its language as a result of the process of education and language instruction which Kaspar has gone through. They are all Kaspars. They now only have one language available to them, and this is reduced to articulations of power; one only has to say "uh" to fix something. At the end of this long, dumb scene, the whole company leaves the room. A girl leaves her doll behind and she comes back to fetch it. The miracle that had been expected has not taken place; Kaspar did not speak, although he was asked to do so several times, he was given presents, and sacrifices were made. The girl is alone with this icon Kaspar for the first time and she would also like to experience this miracle. For a moment the girl and Kaspar are in contact, although nothing happens; Kaspar of course does not speak. So she decides to go up close to his body and to touch his mouth, as if she were trying to feel the materialisation of speech. The girl feels Kaspar's breath, but she does not know what speech is. Then she offers Kaspar her doll. She places it on the altar which Kaspar is squatting on, and goes off. This moment moves me greatly when I watch it. It tells me a great deal, I associate it with many things in my childhood. In the world of the Catholic church especially, making sacrifices means giving up what is dearest and most valuable in order to make something good come about. In one brief moment my whole childhood comes back to me, a series of memories and experiences emerges.

*Malgorzata Bartula*: We are now talking about particular moments during performances when a whole world can appear to the person watching.

*Roberto Ciulli*: These are the kind of moments you find in the art of the clown, too; the whole world encapsulated in one small world. I react to such moments with great intensity. I believe theatre lives from the dialectic between a great arc, which an evening in the theatre must have, and the moment which becomes a personal experience for the individual member of the audience. In a microcosm the actor succeeds in embracing a whole world. If a performance which does describe a wide arc does not contain such a moment it will not live. If, on the other hand, I experience a great idea in a personal, microcosmic moment, then the evening has been a success.

*Stefan Schroer*: When I recall some of your performances, it is in fact true that I tend to remember such moments first. And even if I am seeing a performance for the tenth time, this experience still recurs. That is not a moment of surprise.

*Roberto Ciulli*: True. It is not dependent on recognition. During rehearsals I see such moments over and over again for eight weeks, on a daily basis. They repeat themselves, and in fact their quality does remain subjectively unchanged. They always strike the nerve. In the reception you achieve the synthesis between reason and feeling. They are utopian, redemptive moments, where the thinking mind and the feeling body come together. Something is resolved, is offset. When you respond to them you cry. Or you laugh. A strong emotion cannot be repressed, it asserts itself and finds physical expression.

*Stefan Schroer*: There is a scene in *Teatro Comico* which calls forth both types of reaction. Maria Neumann as Forello puts on a performance for the rich Turk who wants to pull down the theatre and ship it to Smyrna. She predicts the apocalypse from the pattern of a woven carpet. When she says: "A fiery dachshund appears in the heavens" the rich Turk corrects her: "That was a dragon, not a dachshund". The actress immediately interrupts her speech and asks him quite seriously: "What do you think you are doing, interrupting me like this? Do you thing I am fooling about? You'll be telling jokes when the world comes to an end. You don't know what 'coming to an end' means".

*Roberto Ciulli*: That particular moment lives from the fact that the actress is stepping out of the theatrical context. The actress is acting theatre, very artificially. As a member of the audience you are involved in this and you accept what happens, but as acting in the theatre. Suddenly, within a fraction of a second, it ceases to be theatre and becomes very personal. One has entered on an agreement that this is theatre, and therefore artificial, and then all of a sudden it changes: Watch out, this is life, this is serious.

*Malgorzata Bartula*: Maria Neumann's scene is clowning, that increases the height of the drop.

*Roberto Ciulli*: She comes on as a clown, as an actress who is often engaged to play the role of a clown. And with clown-like humour she conjures up the apocalypse. The member of the audience responds to the humour of the scene, but she suddenly abandons him in this position. He thinks what he is getting is entertainment, but suddenly it becomes a matter of life or death.

*Stefan Schroer*: Another scene in *Teatro Comico* expresses this more explicitly. At the beginning of the play some pale figures foregather; they were once actors and would still like to be so, perhaps they still are. Then a young woman joins them. Asked who she is, she replies that she is an actress. Suddenly the whole company, which has been quite silent until then, jumps at her, screaming and protesting: "That cannot be, with a face that colour!" An actress pulls out a pistol and says to her: "Now you are going to die." The young woman answers: "I can't, I have never learnt how to die." This answer saves her life.

*Roberto Ciulli*: Logically what is taking place here is an inversion: called upon to really die, she remembers that she is in the theatre. It is this constant dialectic in the theatre that brings me closer to reality, to my reality, than in so-called real life. Sometimes the opposite is the case: when I am in the theatre, I need to take a break from acting. This constant alternation between life and playing theatre creates the kind of moments we have been talking about.

Sometimes they come about by accident in rehearsal, yet they are not really accidents, since what is behind them is the *conditio* of the actor, in the sense of improvisation.

*Stefan Schroer*: At the very heart of the dialectic between such a singular moment and the great arc of a production is a scene in *The Cherry Orchard*. There is a moment which forms the culmination of a whole arc of the production. When it ends, the Chekhov character changes into a more personal one, and it is this that determines the whole of the last act. At that particular moment Anya tries to draw her mother, who has begun playing the piano after Lopachin's announcement that he has bought the orchard, back to reality. First, she stands behind the piano and bends further and further over it towards her mother without reaching her, neither with her hands nor with her words, which become more and more beseeching. Finally she lies right across the piano. When she raises her head again, she is no longer Chekhov's Anya.

*Roberto Ciulli*: That is the kind of moment for me too, where everything that has happened before comes together with a force I cannot escape. I have experienced this in rehearsals too, at least forty times. Which reveals the particular quality of such a moment. You work with an actor on such a scene, you see what has not succeeded, you criticise, yet, nevertheless, this moment gets to you every time. Why is that so? In such moments an abyss opens up in an acting situation you have agreed on and you are pulled straight back into life. It is as though a trap door had opened and you fall through it. Before that, everything had looked quite easy, but suddenly something grips you, you identify completely with the situation and the character on the stage, and you feel a deep sense of powerlessness. You can feel this powerlessness in life, too, and for us this was the moment in *The Cherry Orchard* where the whole acting situation was shown to be real. If I pay attention, I will perhaps realise that what I have just seen has not been a performance of Chekhov's *Cherry Orchard*, but actors who have been using *The Cherry Orchard* to talk about their own lives. The actors have not been performing for an audience, they have been living through their own conflicts – with *The Cherry Orchard* as the score.

*Malgorzata Bartula*: It is clear to me now that the acting situations we have been talking about are related in kind. Although they occur in different stories, they share the same characteristic, a unified substance consisting in an intensification which transcends the separation of theatre and life. And all of them have to do with death and with love. In that same *Cherry Orchard* I am always moved by the moment where Lopachin, who at the end of the day is a nice man and is also right, is threatened with the revolver. That is acted, but just for a moment he really does think he is going to get shot. That is a game the actors play with him, and afterwards he is told: It was only a joke, but when we actors leave, there will not be a soul here. This person is right, he has his way of keeping life alive, but he still remains alone.

*Roberto Ciulli*: What has kept me in the theatre has been experiencing the kind of moments during my work which give you the impression that they also keep you going in life itself. If it were only a question of acting out something, one could do other things and make much more money. But there is something about such moments in the theatre which are richer than what you actually see. Like the final scene of *Margarete Faust* where Simone Thoma comes to the front, looks at the audience and says directly to them: "I feel so hemmed in." There is another moment in the same scene, a moment of clowning which has to do with setting free laughter, where Margarete dresses up a waiter to make him look like the Madonna. When you notice that the only difference between a waiter dressed up and a Madonna lies in the inclination of the head. That is an incredibly liberating moment, because it uncovers a whole world of deceit. I remember a scene in *The Seagull* which achieved a similar effect. There's a point in the text where Arkadina says to her son: "Don't cry!" This scene is always heard in the theatre as a mother's way of consoling her son. In our production Gordana Kosanovic became very aggressive at this point. She slapped her sons around the ears several times and it was once when she slapped him that she told him not to cry. Each time he was slapped the boy cried more and each time he was slapped harder for it. That is a dreadful experience to have to watch. A mother forces her son not to cry because she thinks men shouldn't cry. That is something many sons have been through. And in this brief moment on stage a whole world opens up for such people.

*Malgorzata Bartula*: I would like to come back to the scene in *Margarete Faust* again. That is a moment which is felt and played by the actress in a very intense manner, but it is held for quite a long time, over a whole scene. A young woman at the end of the twentieth century has given the figure of Gretchen, about whose life Goethe tells us virtually nothing, as much life as she possibly can, so that she is no longer merely a figure on whom Faust projects himself. Her scene as Gretchen is ended, but she does not actually go off. That is how the scene opens. She has the idea of turning a barkeeper very quickly into a Madonna simply by using two cloths and an inclination of the head, and she does so to take revenge, to tell her: "You ruined my life for me." Then she goes up front to the microphone she used for her earlier scene and speaks into it: "I feel so hemmed in." Then she comes back to the front again, and that is the moment for me, and she holds Goethe's famous phial of poison out to the audience and says: "Neighbour, your phial." And she drinks from it. Gretchen is judged.

*Roberto Ciulli*: Of course, this scene contains the exploitation of Gretchen that was already there in Goethe, but it also shows how Gretchen has suffered exploitation throughout the history of German theatre. How many young actresses were encouraged to play Gretchen when they were still amateurs, because it was thought this character could only be played this way, and then they were cast out. How many corpses of Gretchens are there lying about in the cellars of German theatres, how many actresses have been damaged for their whole lives by this role, because this character, which is a product of male phantasy, is unactable? That is why I wanted to step out of theatre at this point and demonstrate the kind of problems an actress who is going to play Gretchen has. The logical consequence of this is that we play the dungeon scene using a puppet.

*Malgorzata Bartula*: I remember how violently we argued in rehearsals about whether Simone Thoma should reappear for this scene or not. Most of the moments we have been talking about have in common that they were quite contentious. For instance, the snow in the cupboard that falls on the old servant Firs at the end of *The Cherry Orchard*. You struggled long over that scene.

*Roberto Ciulli*: You always get a particular type of conflict over final scenes. Perhaps that is because as far as the conception of such a scene is concerned I am always ahead of the actors, because as an outside observer I am able to see sooner how the various elements are connected. I always wait a long time before deciding on an ending, and actually it always remains open, because the life on stage has become so rich that one cannot simply close it with a single image. What interests me about the final scene is how one can use it to take the greatest possible step forward. A final scene which fits a production like a lid is silly. On the contrary, it must shoot an arrow as far forward as possible. And that is where you often get a gap between me and the actors, because at this point I say: it doesn't matter whether it emerges logically from what we already know, we now have to radicalise our imaginations. The last time we encountered such a situation was in *Bürger Schippel*, a play in which the middle class is criticised for its narrow bourgeois values but nonetheless appears harmless enough. We had the bastard Schippel, the outsider who has all the while been struggling to gain their recognition, played by Ferhade Feqi and in the final scene we portrayed the society as the Ku Klux Klan. I open my visions for discussion, but in the end I always want to decide in favour of the perspective which reaches furthest.

*Stefan Schroer*: In my experience the final scene of *Pinocchio* is a good example of the kind of advantage you have over others in the rehearsal process. I resisted this scene for a long time, because for me the arrow you shot forward defied all logic. Two people struggle for influence over Pinocchio for a whole evening but at the point where he approaches them, they completely disregard him. And without them noticing, he leaves them, he flees without aid out of the belly of the whale which he had not previously seemed to be able to find a way out of. This final scene is the exact opposite of bringing something to a conclusion. And in this way, against my inner resistance, one of those scenes which we have been talking about came about. You were particularly involved in the development of this final scene, it could not simply be improvised out of the lives of the characters as they had been developed. The gap you mentioned got in the way, so you must have been directly involved in the improvisation.

*Roberto Ciulli*: If during the course of the rehearsals we have developed many story lines and worked out an inner logic for the story, a logic will emerge for the ending out of what we have done. What is important here is a hypothesis which goes beyond the logical conclusion. The natural ending would be for Pinocchio to end in the belly of the whale, this realm of death is where we all finally end up. It would be a pre-Christian world, like the kingdom of death the Greeks had. But yet this is a Christian world, with a God and a devil, and we are describing this world as a petit bourgeois one, as a world of the family which we have all known from childhood. Like the father, God is watching television and he says to the child: don't pester me. But Pinocchio is also a hero. And a hero like him doesn't end like that, he succeeds in escaping from this place in spite of everything. He manages to do it when he suddenly comes across a book – and this is not an accident. A whole series of teachers has tried to make him see the importance of reading and the need to learn, but he has never paid any attention to them. All of a sudden, when no one is bothering about him, he comes across a book and he becomes interested in it. He realises that he does have a future. Through this book he finds the strength to escape a world no one has ever escaped from before.

*Malgorzata Bartula*: The final scene in the Pinocchio section tells of the end of childhood. In your version that sounds so optimistic, but the scene is cruel to watch. A book saves him from final isolation.

*Roberto Ciulli*: I reject the bourgeois family structure. My best father was not my natural father and my best childhood was not my real childhood. Perhaps the meaning of a good education is that the child is being prepared to question the family without too much pain and to free himself from it. To realise that the isolation which follows is no greater and no smaller than that within the family. The decisive thing is the awareness of the freedom one has to enter on relationships voluntarily. This is necessary work which is not carried out within the given, hereditary structures of relationships or functional relationships. Such questioning is repressed, people are anxious about the consequences. A child would says it wants a different mother.

*Malgorzata Bartula*: We are inevitably returning to talking about final scenes, which you maintain are your avant-garde. The ending of *The Servant of Two Masters*, where two powerless people free themselves from dependent relationships and in a humorous fashion embark on lives of their own also provoked a violent argument in the ensemble. How do you interpret this scene yourself?

*Roberto Ciulli*: It is very strong, because of the *commedia dell'arte,* which it quotes. Two characters appear on stage wearing the costumes of Smeraldina and Truffaldino. That is not unrealistic, since the story takes place in Venice. They come as avengers, not as comedians, and they engage in a real fight. They finish off two old, degenerate corrupters of society whose sole aim was to achieve power and deal in drugs. I feel sympathy for these characters if for no other reason than that as an Italian I was always identified with the harmless *commedia dell'arte* – and what we witness here is: Be careful! You have not understood *commedia dell'arte*! In my other *commedia* performances – and there have been several of them – I have always tried to put this across. C*ommedia dell'arte* was a great revolution of the people against religion, the nobility, the grand bourgeoisie. It meant terror. There were the first obscenities on stage and other unheard-of things. If I decide to direct the most typical of all *commedia dell'arte* plays again – a play I have done three times in the classical manner before and each time what I hear is: Yes, Ciulli knows how to do that, he should do nothing but that – I derive great satisfaction from getting away from the tradition and creating a final scene as a *tabula rasa* with the original characters as avengers. At the same time, however, what we also managed to do – and this is what caused the debate in the ensemble – was to formulate a rejection of drugs. A great number of young people came to see this performance and what they experience in the final scene is how these two avengers slice open the packets of cocaine and scatter them to the wind. Away with it, we don't need it. The argument against it was that it was too naïve. I do not see drugs as all black and white, I do not disparage them and, of course,

I could talk about them in quite a different way. But at a time when so many young people have fallen victim to drugs, it seemed to me right to portray two *commedia dell'arte* characters, a man and a woman wearing each others' costumes, struggling for a world without drugs.

*Malgorzata Bartula*: But they keep the case full of money, don't they...

*Roberto Ciulli*: Of course they take the money away with them, they should too because they have earned it.

*Stefan Schroer*: This final scene is a parallel to what you have been saying about other final scenes: it contains a leap forward and a new beginning. A new story begins, then the curtain goes down. That's what happened in *Teatro Comico* too, only that there it was not one or two characters who destroyed or left a place which is dead and the people who inhabit it, but a shared new start takes place. The ship they have been longing for does not have to be sought any longer, it is already there, it is already moving.

*Malgorzata Bartula*: A miracle takes place!

*Stefan Schroer*: This scene is so openly emotional, almost sentimental, that as a critical observer one has to ask why one is nonetheless gripped by it each time.

*Roberto Ciulli*: The secret lies in the miracle. Of course it is sentimental, but that is what we all want, a miracle. One is in a situation where one believes there is no way out. Suddenly everything is changed, it's a miracle. What does sentimental mean? How often have I heard actors and other people use the term, and every time it is like being stabbed. You pass out when you hear such an accusation. What does the term mean? That I am stupid? One should look at why it is being used in a differentiated way. What is felt, what is being implied? Many people confuse a moment where they are emotionally moved with kitsch, and since they do not want kitsch, they reduce the value of the moment that has been created by dismissing it as sentimental, it has to go. Kitsch is false, but I do not have any problems with genuine emotion.

*Malgorzata Bartula*: The high points which have been referred to in this conversation quite clearly have something in common, which is that the question as to the relationship between the theatre and life and thus the separation of the two does not apply. We have referred to moments where actors have stepped out of and then back into acting. There are scenes, which remain very powerful without this, such as the madness of Elena in Eduardo de Filippo's *Schwesterlein, Brüderlein*, the one-act play which concludes the first part of your production *After Admittance No Beginning* [*Nach Einlaß kein Beginn*] . A high point of feeling is asserted at this point and maintained as a plan for life without anyone stepping out of their role. It is the same in the marriage scene between the girl with the blue hair and Pinocchio, where love beyond the grave and till the end of time is expressed in a childlike, naïve manner. That, too, is an absolute moment, where the audience experiences how actors really are what they act.

*Roberto Ciulli*: That means that each true moment can be experienced. At the level of intellectual discourse truth is hard to comprehend – there are so many possible truths. When you work on a production what takes place is also an intensive search for objectivity. In the end, however, what matters in the theatre is the moment of truth. The sense of the genuine is something absolute and questions as to sentimentality or a lack of logical coherence become unimportant. These moments cannot be criticised because with them one is moving onto a plane which is removed from such criticism. What is true, is life. Whether it is right or wrong does not matter. It is life. Period. If we succeed in creating moments of truth, then other moments of truth will also emerge, because the audience has also experienced something genuine itself. In my work I am interested only in such connections between actors and audience. In *After Admittance No Beginning* there are very many moments like this. The man dying in bed who cannot die and is full of fear, who watches his sister dancing with his best friend and sees both of them go off dancing to sleep together, and he remains behind alone in the room. He recalls the most amusing moments in his life, and he suffers. One might say: So what? He is only thinking about sex and weeping because he can't do it any more. That is sentimental, and it also seems repugnant. But nonetheless it is an aspect of life that you cannot simply wipe away. It is pointless saying that it is kitsch.

*Malgorzata Bartula*: In the first part of your *Faust* Trilogy Mephisto is a woman. This decision and the way it is transposed in the performance gives rise to a new context and unexpected experiences for the audience, which we definitely ought to talk about.

*Roberto Ciulli*: Indeed. Mephisto is a woman. That means that Mephisto comprises both principles – the male and the female – but the best side, as with all of us, is the female. In *Faust* there is the passage where Mephisto says of Faust: "I'll drag him through the wildness of life." In two hundred years of *Faust* reception we have heard the line so often, always played lustily, as much as to say that: "so, now I can finish him off." When Simone Thoma played this scene for the first time, this thought generated a great deal of pain. And we only had this idea because it was Simone Thoma playing the scene as a woman.

*Malgorzata Bartula*: She despairs of Faust.

*Roberto Ciulli*: True, she does. Mephisto mourns the fate of humanity.

*Malgorzata Bartula*: One watches the scene and one witnesses Mephisto's powerlessness, which is the powerlessness of the woman playing him as well. Weakness, powerlessness, helplessness in the face of this intolerable, greedy, insatiable being who is incapable of lingering. In rehearsal it was felt to be genuine, it caught the theme perfectly.

*Roberto Ciulli*: That is how important moments arise. At that point I came to understand a lot about Mephisto, and I believe, everyone else will feel the same way.

*Malgorzata Bartula*: In the second part of the Trilogy, in *Margarete Faust*, Faust dissects Mephisto's body in order to investigate the essence of evil. He rummages about in his intestines while he speaks the lines from the *Walpurgis Night (Walpurgisnacht)* describing the landscape.

*Roberto Ciulli*: That is a passage where what I am thinking is: watch this and you will see how great the difference is between literature and theatre. And how unjustly people treat the theatre. How many people, how much cultural activity, how much education and how many educational institutions do we require to explain every line in literature. What kind of a relationship is there to what the theatre can and does do with these lines. We are not the only ones who think like this. There were many before us who have worked in the theatre like this, who have breathed life into literature and who proved a stimulus for society. But how little encouragement there is actually to go to the theatre. Let me give you some advice, says Büchner in *Danton's Death (Dantons Tod)*, go to the theatre. A scene like the *Walpurgis Night*, which is actually one of Goethe's weakest but has been most analysed and commented on, emerges as very strong in performance because what it tells us is that Mephisto is the inverse of Christ, he is the incarnation of all evil. He lands on the operating table and what we then experience is not an external description of nature but a vision of the inside of Mephisto's body, where the natural description is transposed to the human body: there are the veins, the ribs, there is the blood. Theatre possesses such immeasurably creative possibilities when compared to literature. The question is only, how does one free oneself from traditional images and enter onto something new, hitherto unknown?

NINTH CONVERSATION

# A Global Effect

*Roberto Ciulli*: In our work we are always meeting new people whose political thinking is moving in the same direction as ours, but who are active in quite different sectors. This difference in spheres of work should not be regarded as an obstacle to the effectiveness of a common idea but as an opportunity, since there are no longer any issues which can be solved exclusively within one field of social activity. In a parliamentary democracy you can found a political party where people holding similar ideas can come together. But developments in technology and in the media are moving so rapidly that we can hardly keep up with them, and this relegates such coming together to the margins. Yet at the same time this development opens up other possibilities of communication between people and, thus, new possibilities of becoming socially active. When the representatives of the wealthiest states gather in Seattle and determine how the world is to look in the immediate future, which countries are to be granted debt relief and which aren't, whether there will be a crisis in a particular region or not, it is possible today to organise global opposition in advance. Even if this protest movement was not able to effect any direct changes, it was nevertheless incredibly important as a symbolic act, because for the first time worldwide networking enabled hundreds of thousands of people to come together in public to protest against such economic dictates.

People have tried at various times to formulate a decalogue of ethical and political demands which would unify a group of people. The time is now ripe for working in such a direction again. A forum can be created for people all over the world, with the aim of gaining acceptance for particular ideas in all sorts of social spheres. If I intend to become active on behalf of my ideas and I want to get in contact with the world, it is extremely difficult to do so without making use of existing structures. But if a symbol, a space, already exists, where I know I can find people I can link up with, then this essential first step is much easier. Our theatre, both as an institution and with the particular people now working there, could become such a symbol, which would first make people acquainted with one another and then seek to create a global initiative.

*Malgorzata Bartula*: You are describing the next logical step in assembling the forces of like-minded people. But what is the core of what you are trying to communicate?

*Roberto Ciulli*: A charta ought to be formulated to address some basic principles. But it is very difficult to set up a charta which does not simply repeat the mistakes made by political parties, religions, and grand ideologies. It must therefore be very concrete and very specific. What we need is basically a second Enlightenment, since the recent developments in the media lead us – unlike the *Encyclopédistes* who began the work of enlightenment – to believe that we are fully informed, whereas in fact we have lost any concrete relationship to this information and have no real way of assessing it. What constitutes our daily work in the theatre is now in general demand: we have to become concrete again. The principle Beuys formulated that every human being is an artist is such a provocative idea that it takes a clear decision to assent to it. But even this idea must be formulated concretely: what does the opportunity to develop creativity in the theatre, in society, in the work place actually mean? Another principle is the idea of equality, an incredibly important idea, which at the moment is being considerably re-evaluated, particularly in the political parties, in the great popular parties. Equality means equal opportunity for all, it means that there are no great differences between human beings. All European political parties are moving further and further away from this principle of equality. Here in Germany social democracy is no longer concerned with equality based on such a right. If you are talented and have the opportunity you are expected to succeed and, indeed, what matters is that the rich should become richer and the poor should receive no more assistance. In America this principle has already gone a long way, to the extent that the poor are being criminalized. If we think through this idea on a global scale, then what we are concerned with is not equality as falsely understood by the Communists, where individual talent is not regarded as having any value. Nor is it the kind of levelling out which our educational systems produce and for which the usual training of actors provides a good example. But it is a question of equal opportunity and of providing everyone with what he or she needs to live.

*Stefan Schroer:* The *Communist Manifesto* was conceived globally, but it implied a misunderstanding, namely that there was this one manifesto and a few other communist writings which would serve as a guide to political action everywhere and in the same way. The concept of a global society today does not need one central, all-embracing manifesto, if only for the reason that it is composed of various, quite concrete efforts on a regional basis and is rooted in existing practice. What it requires in addition is something to hold it all together, which is why the necessary basic principle perhaps can best be designated by the term freedom.

*Roberto Ciulli*: Yes, what we need is a strategic concept based on what is self-evident – ultimately on the concept of reason, which is why one can speak of enlightenment. And at the beginning this will be communicated much more by human beings themselves than by means of any manifesto. If people think in a similar way they will immediately acquire the right common strategy, it does not take many words. But if you want to set up a chain of people, you also have to have some selection, there has to be a filter which does not let everyone through, because you have to be able to place a great trust in such people. That is the difficult thing, but it also offers a greater chance of coming together not on the basis of a theoretical manifesto but through real life, through real encounters, and of thus creating something which will nevertheless have a global effect.

*Malgorzata Bartula*: In your theatre work what you do may be divided up into various sections. You travel to different countries, you hold seminars, you communicate with others via the internet, but everything we have been talking about begins with this work, with your way of working with actors. What you say to the actors – namely, don't bother to think about the effect – is that what you would like to communicate to the world?

*Roberto Ciulli*: Yes, and that is the reason why in my work virtuosity, the greatest possible technical perfection, is secondary. Criteria such as good and bad don't interest me; what does interest me is whether an actor is true or not in a particular moment. This view not only has to do with theatre, it is rooted in a general dislike of "packaging". This is a political question too. If, in Italy today, a party like Silvio Berlusconi's can emerge, interested only in effect and entirely devoid of content, without any ideas, and if in spite of the fact that everybody knows this such a party can then achieve a degree of approval to the extent that they are able to form the government of the country, this shows how dangerously perverted our perspective has already become. We are living in a consumer society which is achievement-oriented, determined by marketing strategies, where external pressure results only from particular interests, and which is not concerned with the 'What' but only with the 'How'. In the last forty years, for instance, the chemical industry has not brought about any improvement in detergents. If the changes really were such as are advertised for each new product, the dishes we wash would burst apart from all the cleansing power. But it is the same product all the time, the only difference is that it is being sold under a new advertising slogan and in a new packet. And now political strategy works the same way as marketing. The invention of the term "the new centre" is nothing but a strategic invention without any real content. One has to counter this development, and I believe that our audience has understood just that. It has sensed that our work is not about packaging but about content and about challenging each person to break out of the vicious circle of constantly increasing virtuosity and effect.

*Malgorzata Bartula*: At the same time such an appeal is also an invitation to enter on the free space which opens up beyond all the seeking for effect, where something like anarchy becomes possible and each person can experience himself.

*Roberto Ciulli*: At any rate it is a plea to spread the wealth created through individuality in a society. And it makes a plea against any attempt to package individuality straight away, to subsume it under isms or theories. The view which is oriented to the 'How' and not the 'What' enables them at the same time to exercise control over many people. In the theatre such control takes place in terms of the critical categories of literary and drama studies. But what happens if something quite different appears? If at a given moment someone appears who does not fit into the predetermined categories, who has a disturbing effect? Either he is ignored or he is destroyed, if he is not yet strong enough. For such individuality, which is not predetermined, is dangerous. It involves formulating questions and possibly destroying institutions which now seem indestructible, it means making some people who have hitherto felt secure because of their very participation in such institutionalisation feel uncertain about their positions. Of course, that can be unpleasant. But that is the reason why Beuys is unpleasant and why many people in America would like to kill Noam Chomsky because of what he is doing.

What we need in place of institutional associations which render people anonymous is a relationship between human beings based on solidarity and on mutual interest. The opposite, the separation of individuals and groups from one another, is still more common, of course. The new states of Central Asia which have arisen since the end of the Soviet Union, for example, are now intoxicated by their independence. They believe they have gained their sovereignty. But that is precisely their error. People in those countries were sovereign, they were part of a great union and they did participate in a great idea: that of uniting different cultures and different peoples and of exercising solidarity in the name of human ideals. Now they are finding that the idea of the international was a lie. They have not become internationalists, and solidarity does not interest them, it is an empty concept. And since they are not used to being individual people, they are falling into the trap set by the lie of history, nationalism, which asserts they are "Kazaks", "Turkmens", etc.

I am speaking as someone who is cosmopolitan. But I did not imbibe this position with my mother's milk. If I had gone along with my mother's ideas, I would very probably be an authoritarian, stupid, nationalist lusting for power. It is enormously important for everyone to come into contact with the idea of the international. This is possible today, and it is what gives us a completely new opportunity. Hundreds of thousands of people have thought the same before us, only they were not noticed, they did not have such an opportunity. Today it is there, but we also have to become aware of it and change the perspective of our work accordingly. It won't help if we simply go on focussing on the artist, the genius, or the author. We have to debate what is going on in peoples' minds when an idea is formulated by people, by books, by performances, and so on.

*Stefan Schroer*: If I relate what we have been saying so far to your international work, then it does not seem to be a question of developing something in one place and then taking it to another place where you require it be done the same way. You are not developing an internationalist concept either though; you are not seeking a universally valid theatre language which can be understood the same way all over the world, whether it be in Iran, in Uzbekistan or in China. Here, too, we encounter the same tension which exists between the more universal position – which you designate as the idea or the thought, together with its realisation through the senses at particular moments during a performance – and its concrete reception, adaptation, or rebirth at another place however that may take place, over which you no longer have any control and apparently don't want to have any.

*Roberto Ciulli*: In any production we render things in concrete and material terms. What we are concerned with is open communication, the path to communication, where different people from different cultures can reach a result. We know what took place on the Silk Road: trading was carried on and at the same time, although we do not exactly know how, stories were told. People met, they liked one another. And suddenly there appeared the Buddhist, the Christian, the Gnostic, none of whom had been there before. The societies bastardised themselves. This kind of intermingling is still taking place, world wide, although through other means. What we are trying to do with the Silk Road Project is to mount a specific project with people who feel like outsiders in their own cultures and to trace the relationship between different types of outsiders, to bring them together and then see what happens.

An exchange with the countries along the Silk Road is already underway, with Turkey, with Egypt, with Iran and with the countries of Central Asia. The next step will be seminars like those we have already held in Uzbekistan and are planning for Iran. The third stage, which is to take place before the actual journey, ought to be a concrete project in a concrete region. There would be a possibility of doing something like this in Oman. There the actors from the *Theater an der Ruhr* will meet actors we already know from various countries along the Silk Road. There is a real theatre building there in the middle of the desert. This group will live there for three weeks and we will give them a theme to work on. For instance, we want to tell the story of how people from various cultures meet in the desert, where the task before them is to build a tower. The problem is that these people do not understand one another. In the performance, which will be created out of improvisations, we will experience how people who do not understand one another live together, work, eat, sleep, make music. They communicate with one another, but are restricted through language, class differences etc. The tower does not get built, because these people are not able to understand one another across these barriers, perhaps they do not want to understand one another; perhaps there are some among them who work against understanding. At some point a murder takes place, or something exceptional like that. And then they do come to understand one another. The tower begins to rise. We shall perform it over there and then here, and then we shall see what happens. That would be a first concrete test for our project and from that we can get some idea of what the next step should be.

*Stefan Schroer*: Is it your aim, though, to establish a link, a communication between different people, or is it to find a universal language?

*Roberto Ciulli*: No, the question is what political and intellectual response should be made to globalisation. The ruling culture exercises such great pressure that all other cultures are being subsumed under it. All of them are becoming Coca-Cola clichés, we cannot escape that any more. In opposition to this culture, which is spreading, other cultures are asserting and defending themselves. But that cannot be the answer. The answer can only lie in activating a global culture of the like-minded against a global non-culture. Differentiated within itself, but the same in the essence of what unites us. We have to find our way back to the point where we abandoned our own cultures. We have to make this sacrifice in order to gain something which is much more important. People are afraid of losing everything and having nothing left. I am not going to find anything new by withdrawing into my own world, but by going out and linking up with like-minded people. If it were politically or strategically useful for me to go to another country or another culture I would be quite prepared to change my language, my cultural habits and passions – within twenty four hours, like a jacket. The differences between human beings are not genetic. And if one has found something which unites us, these differences become quite insignificant, they no longer have any role to play, they become indifferent to us.

*Malgorzata Bartula*: We have been talking about a second Enlightenment. The first Enlightenment consisted in separating from one another, analysing, encountering one another antagonistically and struggling against one another, with clear terms and identities. The consequence of that has been that the terms 'nation' and 'national sentiment' have become synonymous with territorial claims and with securing one's own economic profit.

*Roberto Ciulli*: The question is whether you are living only in your time or whether you are living in your time but with your mind trained on the future. And now you tell me, whether you really believe that it will matter in five hundred or a thousand years whether or not they have turbans in Oman or whether or not there are different nations. Perhaps there will be one global republic by then and we will all be speaking one language. I am living today, in the present, but what I am interested in is infecting people with the future and working in that direction. Not towards the past. Just imagine, you are advocating an idea which has long been dead.

Whereas you could be working for something – no matter how crazy it is – which you think is what life will be about in the future.

HELMUT SCHÄFER

# Invitation to the Dream

It is not only at night that we dream. The human being's day is also pervaded with dreams and guided by desires which are not fulfilled in reality. For a short while day-dreams may change this reality and happiness may seem within our grasp. Yet after leaping a long way forward the dreamer lands back on his feet with a jolt, his surroundings remain the same, and the sun remains hidden behind the thick cloak of cloud. Schubert's song "Where you are not, that is where happiness resides" rings in dreamers' ears and so they start all over again imagining castles in the air which could be the palaces of tomorrow.

"Where you are not..." – all these unknown places invite us to visit them, they reveal their magic only to travellers, and if you do not set out on the journey you will always suppose that happiness is to be found elsewhere than at home. Dreams and journeys are like brother and sister, the one child cannot manage without the other, the traveller without a dream becomes a tourist who sets up his inner and outer living room in stereotypical fashion at whatever distant place he happens to be, and the dreamer who does not travel will soon adapt to reality as if it were the best of all possible worlds.

The traveller is not always made welcome, the dreamer is not always admired; all too often do they destroy the certainty to which people have adapted, they carry other notions of life in their baggage or they dream of a new, a different world. Conventions begin to waver, what one imagines one is perhaps is not true, everything was an illusion caused by a lack of experience or a lack of imagination: is the reality one thought one was so sure of perhaps the real castle in the air, built on sand and scarcely equipped to survive in the future?

It is on the motives of travellers and dreamers that the art of theatre feeds. The cart being pulled along is one of its symbols. The discovery of unknown places, of remote, frequently past worlds and strange people may be the aim of journeying, yet the theatre finds its way to the heart of the matter when it sets out to search for the continent of the human being himself. "Wonders are many, and none is more wonderful than man." This line from the chorus in Sophocles' *Antigone* suggests what it means to try to track down the mystery of the human being, and an actor must attempt the impossible: the mimesis of a mystery which does not wish to reveal itself.

This view is alien to the world the media have created which surrounds us today, one cannot report about secrets which cannot be revealed. The effort would be in no relationship to the success which the shareholders of the *Zeitgeist*, of the spirit of the times, require. The *homo economicus*, who is currently dominating our species, is more interested in balance sheets and virtual transfers than in puzzles concealed in the innermost depths of the human being. To him the core of the individual appears easily comprehensible, happiness does not brood under a stone waiting to be picked up. Whether a calculable happiness is also a vital one remains doubtful, however. This contrast between the unpredictable vitality which inheres in art and the predictable actions of the social being forms the coordinates among which theatre moves today. At the moment we are right to talk about a cultural erosion which annuls all the normative reasoning of previous centuries, there will be no more traditional biographies, the individual will have to write several if he wants to ensure his survival. This will also bring about change in the subject matter of theatre in the present age. Moreover, it must become the advocate of the lived moment which social time is destroying more and more because it refuses to become predictable. When the curtain opens it must reveal something which has not been seen previously so that the audience can view the world with new eyes.

For the traveller and the dreamer a place is now established which does invite them to linger. The building we moved into as a provisional arrangement in 1981 in order to prepare the performances which would tour cities far and near, was promptly transformed into a theatre by the *Theater an der Ruhr* and it derived its charm from the sense that it was unfinished. Many visitors, including those from abroad, not only settled in here very well but also quickly expressed their regret that they did not themselves have such a space available. The fact that the whole spa complex, which used to be dedicated to the care of the body, was reconstituted as a theatre was based on the view shared by theatre practitioners and politicians alike that the charm we experienced at the start would be short-lived and that, hidden behind a smile, decay would continue. Opening a theatre building in 1997 must be regarded as a political challenge to the spirit of the age, which inclines more to dismantling such institutions and to eroding the traces of human dialogues until the point where they fall silent amid the monotony of a media-dominated world. Founded in 1981, the *Theater an der Ruhr* was designed to provide a model, particularly in terms of its structure, and that has remained unique until today. It has indeed remained an exemplary institution, which invites others to imitate it. And one reason for this is the Theatre's extensive international work, whose influence is to be observed even into the detail of its aesthetic development, since we are convinced that theatre which is successful will discover a language that is universal.

*Lulu (Earth Spirit* and *Pandora's Box)* by Frank Wedekind
Gordana Kosanovic as Lulu
Photographer: Stefan Odry

*Kaspar* by Peter Handke
Maria Neumann as Kaspar
Photographer: Harald Reusmann

*Kaspar* by Peter Handke
Maria Neumann as Kaspar
Photographer: Harald Reusmann

*Teatro Comico* based on themes from Carlo Goldoni
Peter Kremer as The rich Turk
Klaus Herzog as Victor, a Singer
Petra von der Beek as The Woman without Memory
Photographer: Klaus Lefebvre

*The Servant of Two Masters* by Carlo Goldoni
Klaus Herzog as the Professor
Ferhade Feqi as Truffaldino
Photographer: Meinolf Kößmeier

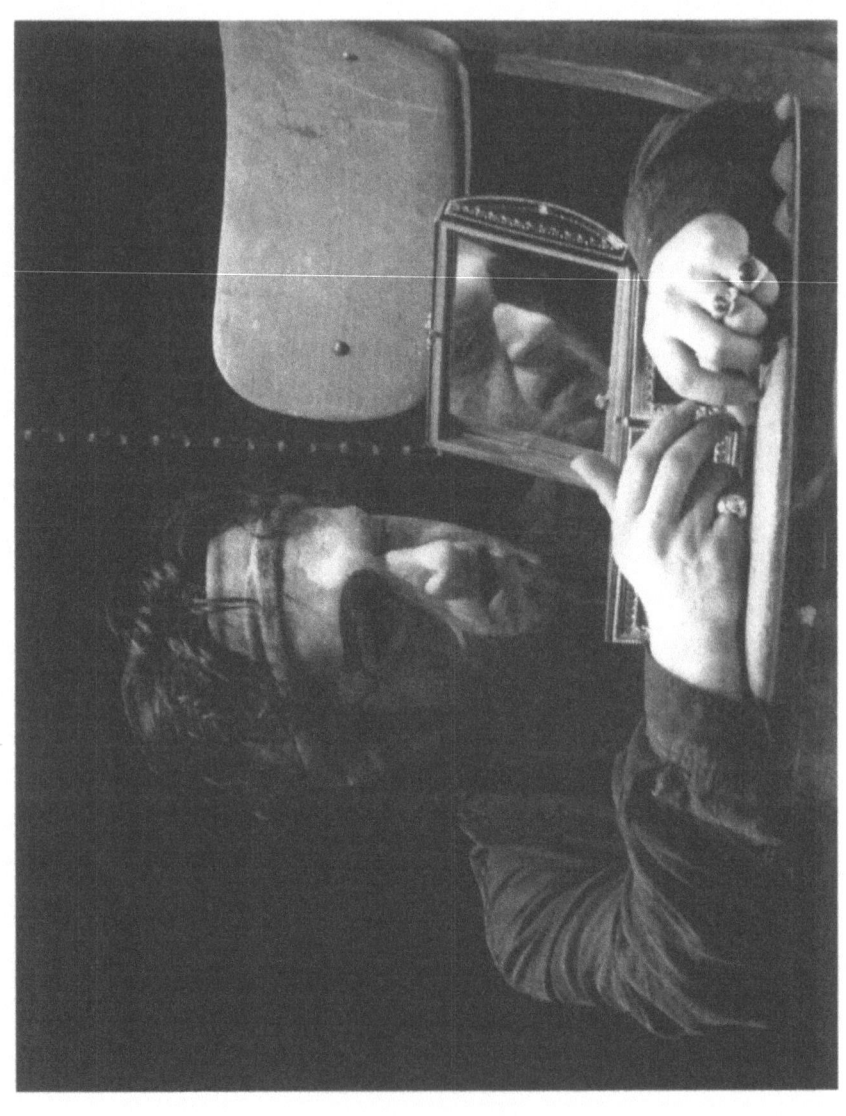

*A Report for an Academy* by Franz Kafka
Ferhade Feqi as Rotpeter
Photographer: Meinolf Kößmeier

*Pinocchio/Faust* by Collodi/Goethe
Petra von der Beek as Monsignore Martinus
Maria Neumann as Pinocchio
Recai Hallac as Brother Silentius
Volker Roos as Peter Rasmus
Thomas Schweiberer as Pater Adelphi

*Pinocchio/Faust* by Collodi/Goethe
Thomas Schweiberer as Pater Adelphi
Simone Thoma as Geppetto
Maria Neumann as Pinocchio
Photographer: Harald Reusmann

*After Admission No Beginning* consisting of five one-act plays by Eduardo de Filippo
Thorten Krohn as Arturo
Thomas Schweiberer as Michele
Photographer: Meinolf Köβmeier

*After Admission No Beginning* consisting of five one-act plays by Eduardo de Filippo

Petra von der Beek as Carolina
David Hevia as Bartolomeo Ciaccia
Thomas Schweiberer as Alberto Califano
Photographer: Meinolf Köβmeier

*Margarete Faust* by Müller/Goethe
Simone Thoma as Margarete
Recai Hallac
Photographer: Meinolf Kößmeier

*Margarete Faust* by Müller/Goethe
Simone Thoma as Margarete
Thorsten Krohn as Faust

ROBERTO CIULLI

# Biographical Data

**1ˢᵗ April 1934**
Born in Milan

**1953-1960**
Studies philosophy at the Universities of Milan and Pavia; completes his studies with a doctorate

**1960-1962**
Founds and manages *Il Globo*, a marquee theatre in Milan, to demonstrate that cultural activities can be located at the periphery of cities

**1965-1973**
Director at the *Deutsches Theater* in Göttingen

Most important productions: *Der Krug* [*La giara*] by Pirandello; *A Midsummer Night's Dream* and *The Taming of the Shrew* by Shakespeare; *Clizia* by Macchiavelli; *Bernada Alba's House* by Lorca; *Les Fourberies de Scapin* by Molière

**1972-1979**
Director at the Cologne Theatre [*Schauspielhaus Köln*]

Most important productions: *Twelfth Night* by Shakespeare; *Ubu Roi* by Jarry; *Six Characters in Search of an Author* by Pirandello; *From Morn to Midnight* by Georg Kaiser; *A Dream Play* by Strindberg; *The Servant of Two Masters* by Goldoni; *The Lower Depths* by Gorky; *The Poor Cousin* by Barlach; *Tales from the Vienna Woods* by Horváth; *Too Many Ghosts* and *Grand Magic* by

De Filippo; *The Knickers, The Snob* and *Das Fossil* [*The Fossil*] by Sternheim; *Cyclops* by Euripides (which won First Prize awarded by the theatre critics at the Thirteenth Belgrade International Theatre Festival, BITEF); *The Cherry Orchard* by Chekhov

## 1974-1977
Guest director at the *Freie Volksbühne* and at the Schiller Theatre in Berlin

Productions: *The Servant of Two Masters* by Goldoni; *Leonce and Lena* by Büchner; *Le Coup de Trafalgar* by Vitrac; *A Man's a Man* by Brecht

## 1979
Visiting professorship at the *Hochschule der Künste* [Conservatory] in Berlin

Project: Ödon von Horváth, *Und die Liebe höret nimmer auf* [And love never ends] with eight trainee actors

## 1979-1981
Director at the Düsseldorf Theatre [*Düsseldorfer Schauspielhaus*]
Most important productions: *Alcestis after Euripides* (Ciulli/ Schäfer) which won the First Prize awarded by the audience at the 14th BITEF-Festival in Belgrade; *The Decameron after Boccaccio* (Ciulli/Schäfer); *März, Ein Künstlerleben* [*March, An Artist's Life*] by Kipphardt; *God* by Woody Allen (first performance in Germany).

In November 1981 the *Theater an der Ruhr* is founded as a limited company. The partners are the City of Mülheim, Roberto Ciulli and Helmut Schäfer. The deed of partnership is limited in the first instance to five years.

## 1981
Guest directorships: *The Decameron 81 after Boccaccio* at the ATELJE 202 in Belgrade; *Medea* by Ciulli/Schäfer at the Stuttgart Theatre [*Stuttgarter Schauspielhaus*]

# THE THEATER AN DER RUHR

## *1981/82 Season*

All productions without any specific attribution were created under the direction of Roberto Ciulli.

**August**
Beginning of the first season, 1981/82.

**November**
First première at the *Theater an der Ruhr*, *Lulu* by Frank Wedekind, in the *Stadthalle Mülheim*.

**December**
Opening of the Studio Theatre at the former saltwater spa in Raffelberg Park with the new production of *Cyclops* by Euripides.

**January**
Start of rehearsals for *Endgame* by Samuel Beckett. In June of the same year the author bans all performances on the grounds that a woman is being cast in the role of Clov. Collaboration with the *Freie Volksbühne* in Berlin on the occasion of guest performances of *Cyclops* over a two-week period.

**April**
Première of the first German performance of Woody Allen's one-act plays *Death* and *God* at the Mülheim *Stadthalle*.

**November**
The theatre sends *Cyclops* to the First North Rhine-Westphalian Theatre Festival [*NRW-Theatertreffen*] in Wuppertal.

## 1982/83 Season

**August**
Tour to the *Freie Volksbühne*, Berlin with Woody Allen's *Death and God*.

**September**
*Cyclops* recorded for television by WDR (West German Radio and Television)

**November**
Première of *A Midsummer Night's Dream* at the Mülheim *Stadthalle*.

**December**
*Wintertagwacht – Texte aus geträumten Nächten (Winter Day Watch – Texts from Dreamed Nights)* from Shakespeare to Ernst Jandl, Première at the Theatre in the Raffelberg Park.

**January**
Première of *Groß und Klein* [*Big and Small*] by Botho Strauss in the Theatre in the Raffelberg Park.

**March**
First German performance of *Der neue Prozeß* [*The New Trial*] by Peter Weiss as a co-production of the *Theater an der Ruhr* and the *Freie Volksbühne*, Berlin.

**April**
The theatre is invited to take part in the First Theatre Festival in Parma with its production of *A Midsummer Night's Dream*.

**May**
Première of *Der neue Prozeß* [*The New Trial*] by Peter Weiss at the Mülheim *Stadthalle*

Invitations to the Nancy Festival and to the Holland Festival in Rotterdam to perform *A Midsummer Night's Dream*.

**June**
*A Midsummer Night's Dream* put on at the Second North Rhine-Westphalian Theatre Festival in Bochum.

## 1983/84 Season

**September**
Invitation to the Seventeenth BITEF with *A Midsummer Night's Dream* and *Groß und Klein*. The Jury awards the prize for the best all-round artistic performance to the *Theater an der Ruhr*.

*A Midsummer Night's Dream* is recorded for Yugoslav television.

*A Midsummer Night's Dream* is performed at the National Theatre in Zagreb.

**November**
Première of *Electra* by Sophocles at the Stadthalle in *Mülheim*.

**March**
Première of *The Seagull* by Chekhov at the *Stadthalle* in Mülheim.

Invitation to take *Electra* to the European Cultural Festival in Karlsruhe

**May**
Opening of the renovated theatre in Groningen with a performance of *A Midsummer Night's Dream*.

*A Midsummer Night's Dream* and *God* are performed at the Culture Circus [*Kulturcircus*] in Nuremberg.

*Electra* is shown during the Third North Rhine-Westphalian Theatre Festival in Paderborn.

**June**
Première of *La Moscheta* by Angelo Beolco, otherwise known as Ruzante, in Berlin as a co-production between the *Theater an der Ruhr* and the *Freie Volksbühne*.

## 1984/85 Season

**October**
Première of *Tartuffe – The Story of Monsieur Orgon* after Molière given at the Mülheim *Stadthalle* in cooperation with the writer Wolfgang Deichsel.

**November**
New production of Ruzante's *La Moscheta* at the Theatre in the Raffelberg Park.

**December**
Ten-year extension of the deed of partnership for the *Theater an der Ruhr* as a limited company until 1996.

**February**
New production of *The Seagull* with Gordana Kosanovic playing Nina, instead of Arkadina as previously, and Veronika Bayer Arkadina, instead of Nina.

**March**
Invitation to the European Cultural Festival in Karlsruhe with *Tartuffe*.

**April**
Participation in the Fourth North Rhine-Westphalian Theatre Festival in Krefeld/Mönchengladbach with *Groß und Klein*.

**May**
Guest performance of *La Moscheta* at the Duisburg *Akzente* Festival.

## 1985/86 Season

**September**
Première of *Kasimir and Karoline* by Ödon von Horváth at the *Stadthalle*, Mülheim.

**October**
Television recording of *Kasimir and Karoline* by the WDR.

**November**
The theatre is invited to the Athens Festival the year the city is European City of Culture. *Electra, A Midsummer Night's Dream* and *God* are performed.

The *Theater an der Ruhr* becomes the first German theatre to undertake a tour of Yugoslavia. *Electra* and *Kasimir and Karoline* are performed in Belgrade, Subotica, Zagreb and Ljubljana.

**January**
Première of *Happy Days* by Samuel Beckett at the *Stadthalle*, Mülheim.

**March**
The theatre is invited to the European Cultural Festival in Karlsruhe with *Happy Days*.

**April**
Première of *Lulu (Earth Spirit* and *Pandora's Box)* by Frank Wedekind at the *Stadthalle* in Mülheim.

**May**
The *Theater an der Ruhr* organises a series of festivals entitled *Internationale Theaterlandschaften* (International Theatre Landscapes), which over a three-year period will present theatre from a different country each year.

The theatre landscape presented in the first year is that of Yugoslavia. Theatres from Subotica and Ljubljana perform in Mülheim.

Above and beyond its theatre work, the Theater an der Ruhr aims to become a place where social and political issues may be addressed. Apart from matinées devoted to the theatre's productions, Roberto Ciulli and Helmut Schäfer regularly host discussions with artists, scientists, and politicians from home and abroad.

*Matinée:* Political Theatre in Yugoslavia and the Federal Republic of Germany Today, with guests from the first "theatre landscape" series, Yugoslavia.

The theatre is invited to the Summer Festival in The Hague and Rotterdam with *Happy Days* and *Groß und Klein*.

**June**
Guest performance at the Fifth North Rhine-Westphalian Theatre Festival in Münster with *Happy Days*.

Première of *Danton's Death* at the Open-Air Festival in Schwäbisch Hall, a co-production.

On 8$^{th}$ August 1986 Gordana Kosanovic dies in Belgrade.

*1986/87 Season*

**September**
*Happy Days* recorded for television by ZDF (Channel Two of German Television)

Founding of the Friends of the Theater an der Ruhr Association [*Verein zur Förderung des Theaters an der Ruhr*]. The Association makes a grant to finance a prize for actors to be named after Gordana Kosanovic, whose work was so important for the aesthetics and for the spirit of the theatre.

**November**
Première of *Danton's Death* by Georg Büchner, at the Mülheim *Stadthalle*.

**December**
New production of *God* by Woody Allen at the Theatre in Raffelberg Park.

**February**
Première of *Morts sans Sépulture* by Jean-Paul Sartre at the Theatre in Raffelberg Park.

**March**
Visit to Ankara and Istanbul to perform *Danton's Death* and *God*.

**May**
Second year of the *Theaterlandschaft* (Theatre Landscape) Festival with Yugoslavia as the focus.

The *Theater an der Ruhr* hosts the Subotica National Theatre with five productions in Mülheim.

**June**
First German performance of *The Croatian Faust* by Slobodan Snajder at the Mülheim *Stadthalle*.

## 1987/88 Season

**October**
Invitation to the Theatre Festival in Parma for performances of *Morts sans Sépulture*.

**November**
Première of Peter Handke's *Kaspar* at the Mülheim *Stadthalle*

The Friends Association of the *Theater an der Ruhr* makes the first award of the Gordana Kosanovic Prize for Acting to Ulrich Wildgruber.

**December**
Première of *The Threepenny Opera* [*Die Dreigroschenoper*] by Bertolt Brecht at the Theatre in Raffelberg Park.

**January**
Première of three cinema trailers for the theatre productions of *God*, *Danton's Death* and *The Croatian Faust*.

**March**
Visit to Yugoslavia for guest performances of *Morts sans Sépulture* in Ljubljana and *The Croatian Faust* in Zagreb and Belgrade.

**April**
*The Croatian Faust* recorded for television by WDR.

Invitation to the European Cultural Festival in Karlsruhe with *The Croatian Faust*.

**May**
Invitation to the 1988 Berlin Theatre Festival [*Berliner Theatertreffen*] with *Morts sans Sépulture* and *Kaspar*.

Third Year of Theatre Landscape Yugoslavia; seven productions from Ljubljana, Subotica and Zagreb are presented in Mülheim. A week-long festival of Yugoslav films takes place.

*Matinée*: Imagination and Variety.

Yugoslav Film makers in Conversation.

**June**
The theatre takes part in the Eighth North Rhine-Westphalian Theatre Festival in Düsseldorf with *Kaspar*. Invitation to the Nuremberg Culture Circus and to the Heidelberg Playmarket [*Stückemarkt*] with *Kaspar*.

## 1988/89 Season

**September**
Première of *The Bacchae* by Euripides at the *Stadthalle* in Mülheim

**October**
Tour to Poland: visiting performances of *Danton's Death* and *Kaspar* in Poznan, Kraków and Warsaw as part of the German Cultural Week Festival [*Deutsche Kulturwoche*].

## January
Première of Samuel Beckett's *Waiting for Godot* at the *Stadthalle*, Mülheim.

## February
The *Theater an der Ruhr* organises a series of readings from Polish literature in preparation for the First year of Theatre Landscape Poland in May 1989.

## March
Invitation to the European Cultural Festival in Karlsruhe and to the Duisburg *Akzente* Festival with *Danton's Death*.

For the first time since 1945 the Turkish State Theatre visits the Federal Republic of Germany.

The *Theater an der Ruhr* organises a tour of their production of Yüksel Pazarkaya's *Mediha* to a number of cities in North Rhine-Westphalia.

Matinée performance: *Mediha* – a guest performance by the Turkish State Theatre.

Discussion with the author Yüksel Pazarkaya and the director Raik Alniacik.

## April
The theatre is invited to perform *Kaspar* at the MESS Festival in Sarajevo. This is followed by a visiting performance in Zenica.

## May
The first year of Theatre Landscape: Poland: The *Theater an der Ruhr* hosts theatres and artists from Poznan, Kraków and Warsaw in Mülheim.

## June
The theatre performs *Danton's Death* at the Ninth North Rhine-Westphalian Theatre Festival in Aachen.

**July**
The theatre is invited to perform *The Croatian Faust* at the Danube Festival, East West [*Donaufest Ost-West*] in Ulm.

The *Theater an der Ruhr* presents a Polish film week at the Theatre in Raffelberg Park.

The City of Mülheim awards the *Theater an der Ruhr* the Ruhr Prize for Arts and Sciences.

## *1989/90 Season*

**September**
The second award of the Gordana Kosanovic Prize for Actors is made through the *Theater an der Ruhr* Friends Association to Veronika Drolc and Miki Manoilovic in Belgrade.

The Theatre is invited to the Twenty-third Belgrade International Theatre Festival, BITEF.

*Kaspar* is awarded the Grand Prix and the First Prize awarded by the Audience, *The Bacchae* takes the Third prize awarded by the audience. The newspaper *Politika* awards Roberto Ciulli the Prize for Best Director for *Kaspar*.

**October**
Première of *Das Käthchen von Heilbronn* by Heinrich von Kleist in Ljubljana. This is the first time a West German theatre organises a première abroad. This German-language performance was the result of a co-production with the *Cankarjev Dom* Cultural Centre.

**November**
Guest performances in East Germany: The Presentation of Art and Culture from North Rhine-Westphalia in Leipzig includes *The Croatian Faust* and *Kaspar*.

**December**
New production with orchestral accompaniment of *The Threepenny Opera* by Brecht at the *Stadthalle*, Mülheim.

Première of *Das Käthchen von Heilbronn* by Heinrich von Kleist at the Stadthalle Mülheim.

Première of *Clowns* at the *Theatre in Raffelberg Park*, a tribute to the art of the clown using texts by Eduardo de Filippo, Karl Valentin and Tristan Remy.

**March**
As in the previous year the *Theater an der Ruhr* organises a tour in North Rhine-Westphalia by the Turkish State Theatre with performances of *Sokullu* by Yilmaz Karaoyunlu.

**April**
On March $30^{th}$ Roberto Ciulli is awarded the highest order for cultural merit, the "Order of the Yugoslav Flag with Golden Cross," for his services to cultural relations between the Federal Republic and Yugoslavia.

*Matinée: Dem Haß keine Chance. Ausländer in Deutschland 1990 [Don't Give Hatred a Chance. Foreigners in Germany 1990].*

Discussion with Thomas Schroer (MP), the writer Yüksel Pazarkaya and Ines Langheim (Mülheim Refugee Council).

On tour in Turkey: Visiting performances of *Das Käthchen von Heilbronn, Morts sans Sépulture* and *The Threepenny Opera* in Ankara, Istanbul and Izmir.

At the Theatre in Raffelberg Park the *Theater an der Ruhr* organises a Polish Film Festival devoted to the work of Krzysztof Kieslowski.

*Matinée*: Discussion with the European film Award winner Krzysztof Kieslowski and Werner Nekes, film director from Mülheim.

**May**
Second year of Theatre Landscape: Poland: The *Theater an der Ruhr* hosts theatres and artists from Warsaw, Kraków and Danzig in Mülheim.

For services to Polish culture Roberto Ciulli is awarded the Order of *"Mérite en Faveur de la Culture Polonaise"*.

**June**
The theatre is invited to perform *The Threepenny Opera* and *The Croatian Faust* at the International Theatre Festival of Chicago.

Première of *Leonce and Lena* by Georg Büchner at the Open-Air Theatre Festival in Schwäbisch Hall.

## *1990/91 Season*

**October**
Première of *Leonce and Lena* by Georg Büchner at the *Volksbühne* on the Rosa-Luxemburg Platz in East Berlin.

Première of *Die Welt hat einen ungeheueren Riß* [There is a dreadful rift through the world] with Maria Neumann performing *Lenz* by Georg Büchner.

**November**
Première of *Leonce and Lena* by Georg Büchner at the Mülheim *Stadthalle*.

*Matinée*: *Ökonomie nach menschlichem Maß* [*Economics on a Human Scale*]

*Discussion with Manfred Max-Neef, the winner of the Alternative Nobel Prize for 1983*

**December**
Première of *In the Penal Settlement* by Franz Kafka. Ulrich Greb, Ciulli's assistant director for many years, presents his own first production.

**January**
With the support of the Ministry of Culture of North Rhine-Westphalia Roberto Ciulli succeeds in setting up the only European Roma theatre, *Pralipe* from Skopje, at the *Theater an der Ruhr* in Mülheim.

The *Pralipe* Roma Theatre premieres *Ratvale Bijava (Blood Wedding)* by Lorca and *Marat/Sade* by Peter Weiss under the direction of Rahim Burhan with great success at the Theatre in Raffelberg Park and then tours numerous cities in West Germany as well as in Holland and Switzerland. This is the first step towards a long-term cooperation between the *Pralipe* Roma Theatre and the *Theater an der Ruhr*.

*Matinée:* The Sinti and Roma in Europe.

Discussion with Rahim Burhan, the director of the *Pralipe* Roma theatre. The *Theater an der Ruhr* visits Warsaw for the second time, performing *Clowns, The Bacchae, Leonce and Lena, The Threepenny Opera* and *The Croatian Faust*.

## February

*Matinée*: Yasar, lebt er noch oder lebt er nicht [*Is Yasar still alive or isn't he?*]

Discussion on the performance by the Turkish State Theatre with the writer Azis Nesin and the directors Kenan Isik and Yüksel Pazarkaya.

## March

For the third time the *Theater an der Ruhr* organises a visit to North Rhine-Westphalia by the Turkish State Theatre. All seven performances of Azis Nesin's play *Is Yasar still alive or isn't he?* are sold out.

*Matinée*: Peace without Conditions?

*In view of the world political situation brought about by the Gulf War the Turkish author Azis Nesin is invited to a discussion together with Albrecht Müller (expert on armaments and SPD MP) and Klaus Bednartz (anchorman, ARD Television).*

## April

Premières at the Grillo-Theatre in Essen and at the *Stadthalle* in Mülheim of Chekhov's *Three Sisters* as a co-production with the City of Essen Theatre.

**May**
Third year of Theatre Landscape: Poland. The visitors are groups from Gardzienice, Danzig, Poznan and Warsaw. At the same time Jerzy Kalina's exhibition on the *Genesis of Solidarnosc* is mounted at the Mülheim City Center underground car park.

*Matinée*: Poland before Capitalism

Discussion with Andrzej Gwiazda, the co-founder of *Solidarnosc*, and Jerzy Kalina on the occasion of the latter's exhibition on the *Genesis of Solidarnosc*.

*Matinée:* Art and Religion.

In conversation with the Polish cleric Krzysztof Niedalkowski.

**June**
Invitation to perform *Kaspar* at the Vienna Festival.

Visiting performances of *Kaspar* in Maribor.

*Matinée*: Questions to Amnesty International.

Discussion with Dieter Overrath, Executive of Amnesty International, and Dr. Nadin Elias, Board of the Islamic Centre in Aachen.

*1991/92 Season*

**November**
Première of *Oedipus Tyrannus* by Sophocles in a new translation by Helmut Schäfer at the *Stadthalle*, Mülheim. This is the opening performance of a month-long festival to celebrate the tenth anniversary of the foundation of the *Theater an der Ruhr*.

The *Initiativkreis Ruhrgebiet* subsidises the "Discover Europe" International Theatre Festival to which the *Theater an der Ruhr* invites two productions from the Slovenian theatre in Maribor, Goethe's *Faust I* and *II* together with Shakespeare's *Hamlet,* and Jean Genet's *The Maids* from the Moscow Satiricon-Theatre.

The Art Porter Jazz Quartet from Chicago gives a number of concerts to great acclaim at the Theatre in the Raffelberg Park.

The NRW Ministry of Culture subsidises the first European Theatre Seminar, which takes place under the direction of Helmut Schäfer and brings together an international group of theatre practitioners, academics and journalists to talk about *Theatre after the End of History*. The proceedings of the seminar are published in two volumes by the felidae publishing house in 1994.

The third Gordana Kosanovic Prize for Actors awarded by the Friends Association goes to Kirsten Dene.

Two books are published by felidae in Essen about the work of the *Theater an der Ruhr*: *Das Abendland versuchen* by Erinnya Wolf and *Die Theatervisionen von Roberto Ciulli* [*The Theatrical Visions of Roberto Ciulli*].

Aided by continuing financial support from the NRW Ministry of Culture the *Pralipe* Roma Theatre is able to continue working in Mülheim under the aegis of the *Theater an der Ruhr*.

## March
At the invitation of the *Theater an der Ruhr* the Belgrade theatre *Jugoslovensko Dramsko Pozoriste* visits Mülheim with the Macedonian director Slobodan Unkovski's production of *L'Illusion Comique*. The performance is very successful and is regarded as a symbol of understanding at a time of violent political conflict.

## April
*Danton's Death*, *Kaspar* and *Morts sans Sépulture* are invited to the IX. Intrernational Theatre Festival in Caracas.

The première of *The Lower Depths/The Exception and the Rule* cannot take place because unionised workers of the city's Department of Works employed at the *Stadthalle* are on strike. For this reason rehearsals continue at a Dutch theatre in Nimwegen.

## May
*Matinée*: A black Truffaldino.

Discussion with Marco Martinelli, director and author of *Siamo Asini o Pedanti* [*We are Asses or Pedants*] during a visit by the *Ravenna Teatro* from Italy.

*Matinée*: The culture of the Indios.

An audiovisual performance by Sergio Maldonado from Ecuador.

*Matinée*: We are subsidising mediocrity.

Discussion with Volker Canaris (Director of the Düsseldorf Theatre), Friedrich Diekmann (journalist) and Ulrich Schreiber (theatre critic).

*Matinée*: Borders closed.

An event organised together with the Mülheim Refugee Council on the planned law on asylum procedures.

*Oedipus Rex* performed at the Eleventh NRW Theatre Festival.

## June
Première of *The Lower Depths with The Exception and the Rule* by Gorky and Brecht at the *Stadthalle*, Mülheim.

## June/July
The *Theater an der Ruhr* undertakes a five-week tour to South America, performing *Danton's Death, Kaspar* and *Morts sans Sépulture*. The places visited are Santiago de Chile, Quito/Ecuador, San José/Costa Rica and the International Theatre Festival in Mexico. This tour is one of the Goethe Institute's largest and most successful enterprises.

## *1992/93 Season*

## November
*Matinée*: Culture against Violence – where is the Federal Republic going?

Discussion with Hans-Jürgen Wischnewski (former minister in the Federal government) and Bodo Hombach (Member of the Provincial government)

"Culture against Violence" is the title of an initiative of the *Theater an der Ruhr* and the *Pralipe* Roma Theatre, which is an appeal against increasing hostility toward foreigners in Germany. Under the slogan "the gypsies are here again" the *Pralipe* Theatre presents its production of *Ratvale Bijava (Blood Wedding)* performed in Romany in about 15 cities in the Federal Republic, including Halle, Hoyerswerda, Lübeck, Magdeburg, Munich and Rostock. The Movement for Another Germany appeals for solidarity and discussion. After each performance discussions with politicians and with the audience take place. The tour, which has been organised spontaneously, is finally supported by the NRW Ministry of Culture and it is greatly acclaimed by public and media alike.

**January**
Première of Shakespeare's *Macbeth* first in Ludwigshafen in co-production with the *Theater im Pfalzbau*, and then at the Mülheim *Stadthalle*. Roberto Ciulli workshops the production together with the film director Hans Peter Clahsen.

Klaus Arzberger, costume designer and artistic director of the *Theater an der Ruhr* since its foundation, dies of Aids.

**April**
*Matinee*: The principle of hope.

In conversation with Slobodan Snajder (the author of *The Croatian Faust*) and Dr. Mladen Cepulic (Children's Hospital, Zagreb) on their support programme for children suffering from cancer in Yugoslavia.

**May**
As part of the first year of the Theatre Landscape: Russia Festival various theatre groups from Moscow and St. Petersburg perform in Mülheim.

*Matinée*: New Departures in Theatre.

*In conversation with journalists, directors and actors from Moscow and St. Petersburg, as part of the Theatre Landscape: Russia Festival.*

**June**
The Twelfth NRW Theatre Festival, which is organised for this year by the *Theater an der Ruhr*, opens with the première of the *Pralipe* Theatre's *O Baro Phani* after Zivko Cingo [The Great Water]. The Roma Theatre gains the prize for the best production.

**July**
At the request of the Minister of Culture and the General Director of the Turkish State Theatre Roberto Ciulli holds a three-week seminar in Istanbul, whose aim is to contribute to the thematic and structural renewal of the State Theatre in Turkey.

*1993/94 Season*

**October**
Commissioned by the *Initiativkreis Ruhrgebiet* the *Theater an der Ruhr* for the second time organises the "Discover Europe" International Festival with productions from Cameroon, Chile, Italy and Turkey.

*Matinée*: Theatre in Africa.

Discussion with Ambrois Mia (actor and director from Cameroon), Bernard Dadie (writer, Ivory Coast), Eric Mambouya (actor and director, Congo).

*Matinée*: Opting out of Industrial Society.

Discussion with Prof. Ulrich Menzel on structural changes in the world economy.

**November**
The premières of *Teatro Comico* based on themes from Carlo Goldoni at the *Stadthalle* Mülheim and of *Veracruz*, based on themes from Euripides, the opening performance in the new per-

formance space in the Roundhouse at Broich Castle [*Schloss Broich*].

*Matinée*: The liberation of the Koran.

Discussion with the literary scholar Nasr Hamed Abu-Zaid (University of Cairo) and Prof. Stephan Wild (University of Bonn).

**January**
For the first time a co-production is set up between a German theatre and the Turkish State Theatre. Working with actors from several places in Turkey and with the director Müge Gürman Roberto Ciulli workshops in Mülheim a production of *Bernarda Alba's House* by Lorca in Turkish.

**February**
The première of *Bernarda Alba's House* by Lorca takes place at the *Stadthalle*, Mülheim. The Turkish ensemble performs in more than twenty cities in Germany by April. The production is then incorporated into the repertoire of the Turkish State Theatre.

*Matinee*: On Lorca.

Lecture and discussion by Fernando de Ita (Theatre critic and writer from Mexico).

**March**
Extension of the deed of partnership of the *Theater an der Ruhr* until the year 2006. A new clause is added to the constitution pertaining to "the cultivation and promotion of national and international theatre art".

**April**
Première of *Hamlet. Act Three* (William Shakespeare), a production by Fred Schediwy, first in co-production with the State Theatre of Baden as part of the European Cultural Festival in Karlsruhe, and later at the *Stadthalle* in Mülheim.

**May**
The third tour to Turkey by the *Theater an der Ruhr* takes the company to Ankara, Izmir, Mersin and Istanbul with performances

of *Macbeth, Teatro Comico, Veracruz, The Lower Depths/The Exception and the Rule.*

Roberto Ciulli is appointed to the position of artistic advisor to the Turkish State Theatre "in recognition of his valuable contribution to international theatre and particularly to the establishment and continuous intensification of relations between the Turkish State Theatre and the Theater on the Ruhr."

Theatre Landscape: Russia, second year. The Klim workshop theatre from Moscow, which had already performed in Mülheim in 1993, presents its *Hamlet*-project.

**June**
While the *Theater an der Ruhr* in the Raffelberg Park is being renovated the Roundhouse at Schloss Broich functions as the residence of the theatre.

## *1994/95 Season*

**September**
Tour of the *Theater an der Ruhr* to three republics of the Commonwealth of Independent States (CIS). The productions of *The Lower Depths* with *The Exception and the Rule, Macbeth, Veracruz* and *Hamlet. Act Three* are shown in St. Petersburg, Moscow, Kiev and Minsk.

In Moscow the *Theater an der Ruhr* Friends Association presents the Gordana-Kosanovic Prize for Actors to the Russian actor Alexander Mesenzev.

The Prime Minister of NRW, Johannes Rau, presents Roberto Ciulli with the Order of Merit of the State of NRW "in recognition of his services to the State of North Rhine-Westphalia and to its population."

**November**
Première of *The Servant of Two Masters* by Carlo Goldoni at the *Stadthalle*, Mülheim.

**December**
*Matinée:* Theatre in Egypt today

With Mohamed Salmawy (author and journalist) and Nehad Salaiha (critic and author) from Cairo.

**April**
Première of Ibsen's *House*, a collage of scenes from Ibsen's plays, at the *Stadthalle* in Mülheim.

Invitation to perform *The Servant of Two Masters* at the Fourteenth NRW Theatre Festival in Bochum.

*Matinée*: *Menschen für Menschen* (People for people).

Discussion with Karlheinz Böhm on his Aid to Ethiopia project.

*Matinée*: "The Silk Road" – a theatre expedition of the *Theater an der Ruhr* using Goethe's *Faust* material.

The first public presentation of the *Theater an der Ruhr*'s *Silk Road Project*. With Roberto Ciulli, Helmut Schäfer, Hans Georg Crone Erdmann (Association of Chambers of Industry and Commerce in NRW), Paul Leo Giani (Italian Christian Democrat), Bodo Hombach (Member of the State Parliament), Heinz Ruhnau (Eastern Europe Advisor of WestLB (West German State Bank).

## *1995/96 Season*

**September**
Première of Brecht's *In the Jungle of the Cities (Im Dickicht der Städte)* in German and Turkish at the Roundhouse at *Schloß Broich*. After his production of *Bernarda Alba's House* the previous year, where only actors from the Turkish State Theatre were involved, the intention with *In the Jungle of the Cities* is to intensify collaboration. German as well as Turkish actors are involved. The problem of translation is not solved technically, but scenically. The production is taken into the repertoire of the *Theater an der Ruhr*. Multilingual performances are to figure in German theatre seasons as a matter of course.

Première of *Turandot, A Class Reunion* (based on Schiller and Gozzi) at the Roundhouse, a production by Stefan Otteni, Roberto Ciulli's assistant director.

**October**
Première of Mozart's *Don Giovanni*, a co-production with the Bonn Opera under the artistic direction of Roberto Ciulli, Gralf-Edzard Habben, Franz Lehr and Helmut Schäfer.

*Matinée*: Lecture and discussion with Freimut Duve on the theme of the war in Bosnia-Herzegovina: Terror against Civilian Society

**November**
An event in support of the People for People Foundation

Karlheinz Böhm reads extracts from Peter Härtling's biography of Schubert.

**December**
*Matinée*: Is there a future for the culture of the Romas in Europe?

Discussion with Heiner Geißler, (Deputy Chair of the Christian Democrat Parliamentary Party), Hansgünther Heyme (Director of the Ruhr Festival, Recklinghausen), Rudko Kawczinski (Association of European Sinti and Roma).

**January**
Première of Don Juan by *Molière* at the Mülheim *Stadthalle*.

**February**
Tour to Sweden – Malmö, Gothenburg, Gävle, Stockholm – with performances of *In the Jungle of the Cities*. In Stockholm the production is shown at the opening of the European Theatre Exchange Symposium, which Roberto Ciulli and Helmut Schäfer participate in as speakers.

**March**
Maria Neumann performs *Grimm's Fairy Tales*. This is the beginning of a tradition, which Maria Neumann has continued since

then with *Snow White, Das tapfere Schneiderlein* [*The brave little tailor*] and *Rumpelstiltskin*.

**April**
Première of *Vorsicht Herz. Blaue Lieder für lausige Liebhaber*. [*Be careful, my heart. Blue Songs for lousy lovers*]. By and with Klaus Herzog and with Mathias Flake at the piano.

**May**
A presentation of the work of the *Theater an der Ruhr* is held at the *Reithalle* in Munich. Within the space of two weeks two performances of each of the six current productions by Roberto Ciulli are put on.

The theatre is invited to perform *Don Juan* at the Fifteenth NRW Theatre Festival in Düsseldorf. Foundation of the *Junges Theater an der Ruhr* under the direction of Malgorzata Bartula.

**June**
Visit to the Dionysia Festival in Veroli and Rome with *In the Jungle of the Cities*.

Guest performances by the Ilkhom Theatre from Tashkent, Uzbekistan, with *Happy Days* by Carlo Gozzi.

## *1996/97 Season*

**September**
For the fifth time the Friends Association of the *Theater an der Ruhr* awards the Gordana-Kosanovic Prize for Actors. The recipient this year is Angela Winkler. Wilson Pico, a dancer from Ecuador, performs at the theatre.

**October**
In recognition of his services to the general welfare Roberto Ciulli is awarded the Order of Merit of the Federal Republic of Germany by the Federal President Roman Herzog. The laudatio states: "As co-founder and artistic director of the *Theater an der Ruhr* Roberto Ciulli has turned the city of Mülheim on the Ruhr into a European

theatre centre. The International Theatre Landscape Festivals initiated by him have brought the wealth of foreign cultures closer to German audiences."

Première of *Die Schlangenhaut (The Snakeskin)* by Slobodan Snajder at the *Theater an der Ruhr* at the Roundhouse in Mülheim.

**February**
A presentation of the work of the *Theater an der Ruhr* at the *Reithalle* in Munich. Within the space of two weeks several performances of the five current productions by Roberto Ciulli are put on.

Première of *Erica P.* by Christine Sohn, a co-production with Kranich-productions, Duisburg, directed by Christine Sohn.

**April**
Première of *The Cherry Orchard* by Chekhov at the *Stadthalle* in Mülheim.

## *1997/98 Season*

**September**
Guest performances at the Festival in Belgrade with *Die Schlangenhaut* and *The Cherry Orchard*.

**October**
Re-opening of the *Theater an der Ruhr* in the Raffelberg Park. The former saltwater spa was the residence of the Mülheim theatre until 1994 and was restored with the financial support of the State of NRW and the City of Mülheim.

Première of *Pinocchio/Faust* by Collodi/Goethe at the Theatre in the Raffelberg Park.

Theatre landscape Post-Yugoslavia: at the Theatre in the Raffelberg Park performances of productions from the Republics of Yugoslavia, Croatia, Bosnia and Slovenia take place.

## November
*Matinée*: Theatre Landscape Post-Yugoslavia: And Now?

*Discussion on the culture and politics in the new republics of the former Yugoslavia.*

## December
For the first time the Mulokot Theatre from Karschi in Uzbekistan and the Tali'a Theatre from Cairo, Egypt, perform at the Theatre in Raffelberg Park as part of the Silk Road project.

## January
As part of the Silk Road project a unique concert by Sufi musicians from the Ne'matollahi-Order in Isfahan, Iran takes place at the Theatre in Raffelberg Park.

A symposium takes place in collaboration with the Evangelical Academy in Mülheim an der Ruhr on the topic: "When God and Man encountered one another on the Silk Road."

*Matinée*: Religious Traditions along the Silk Road: Multiplicity, Conflict and Chaos

A panel discussion with Prof. Annemarie Schimmel, Prof. Hans-Jürgen Klinkeit and Dr. Wolf-Dieter Just.

## February
Première *Love. Women. Brecht.* An Indecent Birthday Serenade by and with Karin Neuhäuser (Voice), Matthias Flake (piano) and Gerd Posny (saxophone, percussion) at the Theatre in Raffelberg Park.

## March
Première of *A Report for an Academy* by Franz Kafka performed by the Kurdish actor Ferhade Feqi.

The *VI. Festival Iberoamericano de Teatro de Bogotá* takes place from the 26$^{th}$ March to 12$^{th}$ April. The *Theater an der Ruhr* is the only German theatre to be invited and performs four plays: Chekhov's *Cherry Orchard*, Molière's *Don Juan*, Brecht's *In the*

*Jungle of the Cities* and *Teatro Comico* based on themes of Carlo Goldoni.

**May**
Première of *Nach Einlaß kein Beginn* [*After Admission No Beginning*] consisting of five one-act plays by Eduardo de Filippo at the Theatre in Raffelberg Park.

**July**
Following on the tour to Colombia, Malgorzata Bartula, Simone Thoma and David Hevia hold a summer seminar on acting and directing theatre at the *Casa del Teatro*.

Roberto Ciulli directs *Dona Rosita* by Lorca at the *Residenztheater* in Munich.

## *1998/99 Season*

**September**
The season opens with the international theatre festival *Theatre Landscape: The Silk Road* which takes place from 11$^{th}$ to 22$^{nd}$ September at the Theatre in Raffelberg Park. Companies from Iran, Uzbekistan and Syria are invited. For the first time since the Islamic Revolution of 1979 theatre companies from the Islamic Republic come to Germany as part of an exchange programme between the *Theater an der Ruhr* and Iran.

On the occasion of the International Festival for Experimental Theatre in Cairo Roberto Ciulli is honoured for his contribution to the development of international cultural relations by the Minister of Culture of the Egyptian Arab Republic Farouk Husni and the President of the Festival Fawzi Fahmi Ahmad.

Gralf-Edzard Habben is a member of the jury at the International Festival for Experimental Theatre in Cairo.

*Matinée*: Theatre Landscape: The Silk Road.

*Discussion with Adurachman Abdunasarov (Uzbekistan), Bahram Beyzaie (Iran), Nabil Haffar (Syria), Sirus Kahurinejad (Iran), Awni Karounmi and Navid Kermani.*

The *Landesverband Rheinland* awards the *Rheintaler* to Roberto Ciulli for services to multinationalism and peaceful coexistence between different peoples in the field of culture in the Rhineland.

## October
Both the *Theater an der Ruhr* and the *Pralipe* Roma Theatre are invited to the International Theatre Festival MESS '98 in Sarajevo; *The Cherry Orchard* and *Yerma* are given.

The *Theater an der Ruhr* performs *Pinocchio Faust* at the El-Salaam Theatre in Cairo, Egypt.

The *Pralipe* Roma theatre is awarded the Lorca Prize of the International Mediterranean Theatre Institute in Fuentevaqueros (Spain). At the same time the *Pralipe* Roma Theatre's commitment to opposing xenophobia is recognised.

## November
A symposium is organised in cooperation with the Evangelical Academies of Iserlohn and Mülheim an der Ruhr, whose topic is "Faust on the Silk Road. The Longing for the West-Eastern Divan."

Première of *Margarete Faust* by Müller/Goethe at the Theatre in Raffelberg Park.

## January
The *Theater an der Ruhr* becomes the first German company since the Islamic Revolution to visit Iran; it takes part in the Seventeenth International Theatre Festival Fadjr in Teheran. Between January $27^{th}$ and February $5^{th}$ 1999 the Mülheim ensemble mounts three of its productions: *The Cherry Orchard*, *A Report for an Academy*, and *Pinocchio Faust*. At the conclusion of the Festival Roberto Ciulli is awarded the Special Prize for Achievement in Theatre Arts and Cultural Understanding by the Iranian Minister of Culture Mohadjerani.

## April

Seven theatre evenings on the theme *Toward Eternal Peace* are put on at the Theatre in Raffelberg Park in response to the war in Kosovo.

## May

The *Junges Theater an der Ruhr* shows the results of its work so far for the first time in public: *Bobok. Szenische Fragmente* [*Scenic Fragments*] and *Faith, Love, Hope* by Ödon von Horváth.

The *Theater an der Ruhr* takes *In the Jungle of the Cities* to Ankara and Istanbul.

*Matinée*: Faust and the Germans.

Discussion with Willi Jasper (academic and writer).

## June

The Almaty German Theatre Academy from Kazakhstan performs *Glücksfelder* [*Fields of Happiness*] by Ingrid Lausund at the Theatre in Raffelberg Park.

At the invitation of the *Theater an der Ruhr* the Yugoslav Dramatic Theatre from Belgrade puts on the *Belgrade Trilogy* by Biljana Srbljanovic and the Centre for Cultural Decontamination shows the *Eva Braun Monologue* in Mülheim between the 6$^{th}$ and the 9$^{th}$.

*Margarete Faust* performed by the *Theater an der Ruhr* is awarded the main prize for the best production at the Eighteenth NRW Theatre Festival in Paderborn.

Kafka's *Report for an Academy* performed for the first time in Turkish by Ferhade Feqi is put on at the Writers' Theatre Festival in Karschi, Uzbekistan.

David Hevia holds a second summer seminar for actors and directors in cooperation with the *Casa del Teatro* in Bogotá, Colombia.

Roberto Ciulli directs *Deutschland, bleiche Mutter* [*Germany, pale Mother*] by Helma Sanders-Brahms at the *Residenztheater* in Munich.

## 1999/2000 Season

**September**

On the occasion of the reopening of the Historical Gardens in the Raffelberg Park an open-air performance of Molière's *Don Juan* takes place.

In collaboration with the Evangelical Academies of Iserlohn and Mülheim a symposium on *Cultural Exchange or Cultural Boycott? Which will benefit human rights?* is organised.

*Matinée:* Cultural Exchange or Cultural Boycott? Which will benefit human rights?

*Dr. Wolf-Dieter Just (Evangelical Academy of Mülheim) and Helmut Schäfer in conversation with Gerhard Baum (Head of the German Delegation to the UN High Commission for Human Rights from 1993 to 1998), Dr. Roberto Ciulli and Faradsch Sarkouhi (Iranian writer).*

Première of *Bürger Schippel* [*Citizen Schippel*] by Carl Sternheim at the Theatre in Raffelberg Park.

Companies from China, Iran and Turkey appear as part of the *Theatre Landscape: The Silk Road* project from 13$^{th}$ September to 2$^{nd}$ October.

*Matinée*: Film, Theatre and Politics in Turkey

*Discussion with artists from Turkey.*

Reading: New Turkish Literature with Kucük Iskender, Perihan Magden and Feridun Zaimoglu.

Award of the 1999 Gordana-Kosanovic Prize for Actors to Slobodan Bestic (Belgrade).

**December**

Revival of *Kaspar* by Peter Handke at the *Theater an der Ruhr* in the Raffelberg Park.

**January/February**
Between 26th January and 5th February: the *Theater an der Ruhr* visits Iran for the second time to take part in the Eighteenth International Theatre Festival Fadjr in Teheran. *Kaspar* by Peter Handke, *Bis die Jahrtausendwende uns scheidet* [*Till the turn of the century us do part*] by Manuel Vázquez Montalbán and *Snow White* by the Brothers Grimm are performed. For the second time Roberto Ciulli is awarded the Special Prize for Achievements in Theatre Arts and Cultural Understanding.

**March**
Visiting performance of Gogol's *Marriage* by the Dramatic Theatre from Grozny, Chechnya.

*Matinée*: *Irrwege der Zivilisation* (Is Civilisation on the Wrong Track?)

*Muchtar Schachnov in conversation with Friedrich Hitzer, Roberto Ciulli and Helmut Schäfer.*

**April**
Première of *Antigone* by Sophocles at the *Theater an der Ruhr*.

**June**
As part of the Second International Theatre Festival in Karschi, Uzbekistan members of the ensemble of the *Theater an der Ruhr* hold a seminar in association with the Theatre Mulokot on founding a multinational Central Asian theatre.

*2000/2001 Season*

**September**
Première of *Der kleine Prinz (Le Petit Prince)* by Antoine de Saint-Exupéry, with Maria Neumann and Roberto Ciulli.

Première of *Schweinestall (Pigsty)* by Pier Paolo Pasolini under the direction of Friederike Felbeck, who has been working with Roberto Ciulli for many years.

## October

Under the slogan "Mülheim Open City" the *Theater an der Ruhr* organises *Theatre Landscape: Central Asia, Kazakhstan and Iran* with performances by companies from Uzbekistan, Kyrgyzstan, Tajikistan, Kazakhstan, Turkmenistan and Iran.

*Matinée*: Theatre Landscape: Central Asia and Kazakhstan.

*Discussion with directors from the theatres invited.*

*Matinée*: Theatre Landscape: The Silk Road and Iran.

Discussion with directors and actors from Iran.

Roberto Ciulli is awarded the *Rheinischer Kulturpreis 2000* (the Rhine Cultural Prize for 2000) by the *Sparkassen-Stiftung zur Förderung rheinischen Kulturgutes* (Savings Bank Foundation for the Promotion of the Culture of the Rhine area).

## November

Première of *The Merchant of Venice* by Shakespeare at the *Stadthalle*, Mülheim.

## January

For the third time the *Theater an der Ruhr* visits Iran to participate in the Nineteenth International Theatre Festival *Fadjr* with performances of *Antigone* and *Le petit prince*.

In collaboration with the Evangelical Academy of Mülheim the *Theater an der Ruhr* organises a conference on the topic: Alliance for Culture? Who foots the bill for culture in a civilised state?

*Matinée*: Alliance for Culture? Who foots the bill for culture in a civilised state?

*Helmut Schäfer and Wolf-Dieter Just (Evangelical Academy of Mülheim) in conversation with Armin Brux (NRW Ministry of Culture), Marion Schneider (Cultural Foundation of the Deutsche Bank) and Roberto Ciulli.*

Festival to mark ten years of the *Pralipe* Roma Theatre. The *Pralipe* Roma Theatre celebrates the tenth anniversary of its foundation with performances from its repertoire, a concert, an exhibition and panel discussions.

*Matinée*: *Pralipe* Roma Theatre – ten years Experience in Germany. A discussion with Rahim Burhan.

*Matinée*: The Roma in Literature – Literature of the Roma.

Reading and Discussion with writers from Italy, Finland, Hungary, and Germany.

**February**
*Matinée*: Shakespeare in Mülheim, Sophocles in Teheran.

Visit to Mexico City to perform *Le petit prince* and *Till the turn of the century us do part* by Manuel Vazquez Montalban at the *Teatro Santa Fe*.

**March**
Roberto Ciulli and the Director of the Theatre and Film Dept. of the Iraqi Ministry of Culture sign a declaration of intent in Baghdad with the aim of organising theatre exchanges between the *Theater an der Ruhr* and Iraqi theatre companies.

**April**
Tour of the capitals of Uzbekistan, Kyrgyzstan, Kazakhstan and Turkmenistan with *Kaspar*.

**May**
Première of Brecht's *Threepenny Opera* (with orchestra).

## *2001/02 Season*

**September**
The Theatre Landscape Festival Iran takes place at the Theatre in Raffelberg Park from 22$^{nd}$ to 30$^{th}$ September with four Iranian theatres and a Tazieh-group participating.

## October

On the 12th October the première of Maria Neumann's adaptation of *Woyzeck* under the title *Der Mond Ist Wie Ein Blutig Eisen* [*The Moon Is Like A Bloody Iron*] takes place.

The première of Carlo Goldoni's *Die Trilogie der Schönen Ferienzeit* [*The Holiday Trilogy*] takes place on the 31st at the *Stadthalle*, Mulheim.

## November

The month is dominated by the festival held to celebrate "Twenty Years of the *Theater an der Ruhr*". Performances are given by visiting companies from Holland, Iraq, Italy, Kazakhstan, Kyrgyzstan, Turkmenistan and Yugoslavia.

On the 25th, the 2001 Gordana Kosanovic Award for Acting goes to Narges Hashempour (Iran) and Anna Mele (Turkmenistan).

## December

Friedrike Felbeck's production of Wallace Shawms' *Marie und Bruce* [*Marie and Bruce*] is premièred on December 15th at the Theatre in Raffelberg Park.

On 6th and 7th the Mexican *Perro Teatro* visits with performances of Lorca's *The Audience* and *Play without a Title*. The direction is by David Hevia who was an actor with the *Theater an der Ruhr* for many years.

## January

From the 21st to the 26th of the month the *Theater an der Ruhr* mounts a festival entitled *Unruh* [*Unrest*], the First Festival of Youth Theatre Groups of the Theatres of the Ruhr Area. It is organised in collaboration with the *Theater Dortmund*, the *Schauspielhaus Bochum* [Bochum Playhouse], the *Westfälisches Landestheater Castrop-Rauxel* [The Westphalian Provincial Theatre at Castrop-Rauxel], the *Schauspiel Essen* [Essen Theatre], the *Theater Hausen*, and the *Ringlokschuppen e.V.* [Roundhouse Theatre] in Mülheim.

In cooperation with the Iranian Ministry of Culture Roberto Ciulli workshops a production of Lorca`s *Bernarda Alba's House* in

Teheran. The première takes place at the *Fadjr* Festival on January 27$^{th}$.

Roberto Ciulli receives the Edita and Ira Hiroshima Foundation Award in Stockholm. The award is in recognition of his commitment to international cultural cooperation and international understanding.

**February**
On the 22$^{nd}$ of the month the première of Susanna Enk's production of Schiller's *Die Räuber* [*The Robbers*] is given at the Theatre in Raffelberg Park. It is the first production by the *Theater an der Ruhr* which works entirely with guests.

**March/April**
Roberto Ciulli and the *Theater an der Ruhr* receive the World Theatre Day Award 2002 from the International Theatre Institute.

From March 24$^{th}$ to April 5$^{th}$ the Theater an der Ruhr performs *Antigone, Kaspar, Le petit prince* and *The Threepenny Opera* at the Al-Rashid Theatre in Baghdad (Iraq).

April 18$^{th}$ sees the première of *Simone Thoma spielt ÄTNA* [*Simone Thoma plays ETNA*] by Christine Sohn at the Theatre in Raffelberg Park.

*Bernarda Alba's House* by Lorca, the co-production between the Dramatic Arts Centre, Teheran, and the *Theater an der Ruhr,* has its German première at the *Stadthalle* in Mülheim on April 28$^{th}$. The play is subsequently performed in Malmö, Stockholm, Cologne and Berlin.

**May**
From the 15$^{th}$ to the 17$^{th}$ of the month the ensemble of the *Theater an der Ruhr* performs Handke's *Kaspar* at the TRANS/FUSION Festival in Stockholm.

## Dramaturgies
Texts, Cultures and Performances

This series series presents innovative research work in the field of twentieth-century dramaturgy, primarily in the anglophone and francophone worlds. Its main purpose is to re-assess the complex relationship between textual studies, cultural and/or performance aspects at the dawn of this new multicultural millennium. The series offers discussions of the link between drama and multiculturalism (studies of minority playwrights – ethnic, aboriginal, gay and lesbian), reconsiderations of established playwrights in the light of contemporary critical theories, studies of the interface between theatre practice and textual analysis, studies of marginalized theatrical practices (circus, vaudeville etc.), explorations of the emerging postcolonial drama, research into new modes of dramatic expressions and comparative or theoretical drama studies.

The Series Editor, **Marc MAUFORT**, is Professor of English literature and drama at the *Université Libre de Bruxelles*.

### Series Titles

**No.12–** Malgorzata BARTULA & Stefan SCHROER, *On Improvisation. Nine Conversations with Roberto Ciulli*, Brussels, P.I.E.-Peter Lang, 2003, ISBN 90-5201-185-0.

**No.11–** Peter ECKERSALL, Naoto MORIYAMA & Tadashi UCHINO (eds.), *Alternatives* (provisional title), Brussels, P.I.E.-Peter Lang (forthcoming), ISBN 90-5201-175-3.

**No.10–** Rob BAUM, *Female Absence. Women, Theatre and Others Metaphors* (provisional title), Brussels, P.I.E.-Peter Lang (forthcoming 2003), ISBN 90-5201-172-9.

**No.9–** Marc MAUFORT, *Transgressive Itineraries. Postcolonial Hybridizations of Dramatic Realism*, Brussels, P.I.E.-Peter Lang, 2003, ISBN 90-5201-990-8.

**No.8–** Ric KNOWLES, *Shakespeare and Canada: Essays* (provisional title), Brussels, P.I.E.-Peter Lang (forthcoming 2003), ISBN 90-5201-989-4.

**No.7–** Barbara OZIEBLO & Miriam LÓPEZ-RODRIGUEZ, *Staging a Cultural Paradigm. The Political and the Personal in American Drama*, Brussels, P.I.E.-Peter Lang, 2002, ISBN 90-5201-990-8.

**No.6**– Michael MANHEIM, *Vital Contradictions. Characterization in the Plays of Ibsen, Strindberg, Chekhov and O'Neill*, Brussels, P.I.E.-Peter Lang, 2002, ISBN 90-5201-991-6.

**No.5**– Bruce BARTON, *Changing Frames. Medium Matters in Selected Plays and Films of David Mamet* (provisional title), Brussels, P.I.E.-Peter Lang (forthcoming 2003), ISBN 90-5201-988-6.

**No.4**– Marc MAUFORT & Franca BELLARSI (eds.), *Crucible of Cultures. Anglophone Drama at the Dawn of a New Millennium*, Brussels, P.I.E.-Peter Lang, 2002 (2$^{nd}$ printing 2003), ISBN 90-5201-982-7.

**No.3**– Rupendra GUHA MAJUMDAR, *Central Man. The Paradox of Heroism in Modern American Drama*, Brussels, P.I.E.-Peter Lang (2003), ISBN 90-5201-978-9.

**No.2**– Helena GREHAN, *Mapping Cultural Identity in Contemporary Australian Performance*, Brussels, P.I.E.-Peter Lang, 2001, ISBN 90-5201-947-9.

**No.1**– Marc MAUFORT & Franca BELLARSI (eds.), *Siting the Other. Re-visions of Marginality in Australian and English-Canadian Drama*, Brussels, P.I.E.-Peter Lang, 2001, ISBN 90-5201-934-7.

**Peter Lang — The website**

Discover the general website of the Peter Lang publishing group:

**www.peterlang.net**

You will find

– an online bookshop of currently about 15,000 titles from the entire publishing group, which allows quick and easy ordering
– all books published since 1993
– an overview of our journals and series
– contact forms for new authors and customers
– information about the activities of each publishing house

Come and browse! We look forward to your visit!